TREES
of the
WEST

TREES
of the
WEST

MABEL CRITTENDEN

Illustrated by Mabel Crittenden and Jack Popovich

Celestial Arts
Millbrae, California

Published by CELESTIAL ARTS, 231 Adrian Road,
Millbrae, California 94030

First printing: March, 1977
Manufactured in the United States of America

Library of Congress Cataloging in Publication Data

Crittenden, Mabel, 1917-
    Trees of the West.

    1.   Trees—The West—Identification.   I.   Title.
QK484.W34C74   582'.1609'78   76-54183
ISBN 0-89087-131-0

1 2 3 4 5 6 7 8 — 82 81 80 79 78 77

CONTENTS

Preface

The west has the tallest of all forest trees; the densest stands of commercial timber, the oldest *living thing* (a tree), plus the other oldster—the Giant Sequoia and its beautiful relative, the Coast Redwood.

Other giants in the west are the Sitka Spruce, the Douglas Fir, the Sugar Pine, the Western Hemlock and the Port Orford Cedar. These western species are the biggest of their genera anywhere.

The west is a particularly good area for conifers, and fortunately there are many national parks and national forests where they can be seen, hiked among, and camped under. There is also a lovely multiplicity of broad-leafed trees, some with wonderfully intricate shapes and forms, some that are specialized for desert living, and some that have been eagerly planted (and/or improved) by man. The west does not have the abundance of fall-coloring trees that the east has, but there are some here!

This book tries to point up the distinguishing characteristics, the interesting information, the usefulness (including

edibility—indicated by a 😊 in the margin), and the beauty of the *Trees of the West*, for it is well-known that the more you learn about something, the more you truly see and appreciate it. Silhouettes of the trees are included to help you spot and enjoy trees as you travel along by car, bicycle, or foot. The leaves, needles, twigs, cones, and flowers will help you know the trees if you can stop a bit and enjoy them. Take time to see the trees—they're worth it.

Some "trees" that have been included are frequently just tall shrubs, but then you'll find some of them that are bigger and tree-like, so many "tree-like" shrubs are included.

Also, particularly in certain areas, an exotic, a non-native tree, has found its new situation so excellent that it has "gone native." Several of these are included because they are commonly found along back roads, along streams, in the mountains, and when the situation is right for them to escape and flourish in the wild, well—they do. They are grouped in the chapter entitled "The Intruders."

And, to help you decide which tree you're looking at, there is a simple, workable "key" that will lead you to the information on your specimen. You will have to look at it carefully and decide which "clue" fits, and progress to the next clue until you arrive at your quest.

And for the final bow in a tree book, there is a chapter on "How to Grow Native Trees from Seed." These are techniques used by nurserymen to get higher germination rates and/or to speed up germination. Try it—you can be a tree grower!

So look at a tree carefully—look until you really see, follow the clues . . . . .

AND HAVE FUN!

To those who love trees and appreciate their fabulous contributions to life on planet earth.

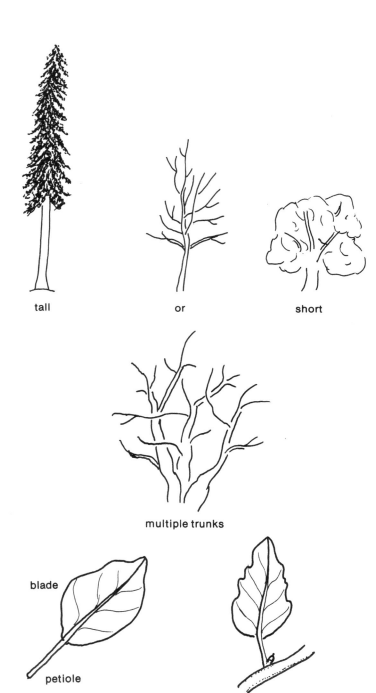

tall   or   short

multiple trunks

blade

petiole

Chapter I

CLUES TO TREE IDENTIFICATION

The more you know about trees, the more you really see them—the forest is no longer just a mass of trees. You'll begin to notice that most forests are not made up of just one kind of tree, but usually of many kinds. Some may be conifers—trees with needle-like leaves or even very tiny leaves that look like scales or small awls. They produce cones of various kinds, and you'll soon realize that not all those "cone-producers" are pines. There may be firs, spruces, hemlocks, and others mixed in. And then you may find that there are broad-leafed trees there also—producing a very different leaf pattern and tree silhouette. Many of these are deciduous and so lose their leaves in the autumn, some of them changing to brilliant oranges, yellows, crimsons and reds before they fall.

As you have realized, trees can be tall or short, conical, as a conifer, or round-crowned, as some oaks. They usually have one main trunk, but many trees either branch very low or have multiple trunks such as the buckeye.

Leaves are made of two parts, the petiole and the blade. Their leaves may be simple, meaning a single leaf is attached to the twig by its petiole. Usually a new leaf bud can be found in the leaf axis.

Leaves may be found in many shapes.

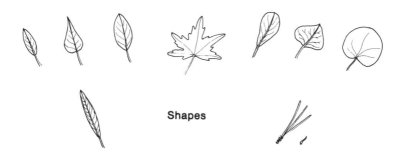

Shapes

And the margin of the leaf may be smooth or variously edged.

smooth   fine serrate   double serrate   toothed   jagged   spiny   lobed

They may have side veins running irregularly from the mid-vein, forming a noticeable network, or the side veins may be parallel to each other. The veins may run clear to the edge (as above) or turn abruptly near the edge and join the next vein—or they may run in many other ways; how many variations can you find. . . ?

netted veins   parallel side veins to edge   side veins turning

Most leaves have just one main vein, with the others branching from it. If it resembles the pattern of a feather, is it called *pinnately* veined (meaning feather-like). There are also some leaves that have more than one main vein. If there are three or more veins of about equal size originating more or less at the same place at the base of the blade, they are called *palmately* veined leaves (since they are sort of like your fingers projecting from the palm of your hand).

pinnately veined   palmately veined

Leaves can also be *compound*—meaning that the leaf is made of several parts (called leaflets). A walnut or locust is a good example. The leaf bud is at the base of the whole stalk, and when the leaf falls, the whole thing falls as a unit. If the leaflets are arranged on both sides of the midvein, and it is

pinnately compound   double-pinnately compound   palmately compound

similar to the feather-like veinage, this is called *pinnately compound* .... And have you ever seen a *double-pinnately compound* leaf? — with each leaflet divided? In that case, the whole leaflet is called a *pinna*, its individual leaflets are called *pinnules*, and the stalk that bears those leaflets is called a *rachis*. Of course, we also have *palmately compound* leaves, as a Buckeye or Horse Chestnut, with the leaflets all originating from the same spot.

Trees can be *deciduous*, which means that they loose their leaves in the autumn. They can also be *evergreen*, meaning that they hang on to their leaves for more than one growing season. Many of the evergreen trees are conifers, holding their needles or scales for many years. These leaves can withstand temperature changes and adverse weather conditions more successfully than broadleaves can. Some of our broadleaf trees are evergreen, as the Madrone and Bay (however, most evergreen broadleaf trees are found in the tropics).

 deciduous winter time   evergreen

You can usually tell if a broadleaf tree is evergreen in that the leaves will tend to be thick and leathery. This is not always true, for some deciduous trees have leathery leaves (such as the Single-leaf Ash). However, if there are leaves from last year's growth besides those from this year's growth, you can be sure it's evergreen.

If trees produce seeds (which most of them of course do, for how else would new ones grow?) those seeds must have developed from fertilized flowers. Because many tree flowers are small and inconspicuous, this book does not often use flowers to help in identification. They are sometimes mentioned, but the fruit is usually more noticeable (and longer lasting) and therefore more useful in identification. Fruit of trees can be tiny seeds in wisps of cotton (Cottonwood), a nut (Walnut), a drupe (Wild Plum), a winged seed called a samara (Ash), a double-winged samara (Maple), a pod (Locust), or an acorn, a nut in a cup (Oak). Fruit can also take the form of tiny woody "cones" (Alders), a variety of woody cones with overlapping scales (Pines, Firs, Spruces), round woody cones (Cypress) or even a cone that has become berry-like (Juniper) with just the tips of the woody scales sticking through the flesh.

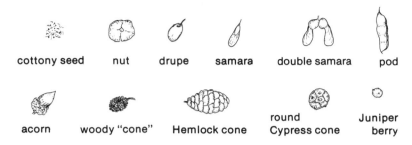

cottony seed   nut   drupe   samara   double samara   pod

acorn   woody "cone"   Hemlock cone   round Cypress cone   Juniper berry

Leaves can also be arranged on the twig in very different (and characteristic) ways.

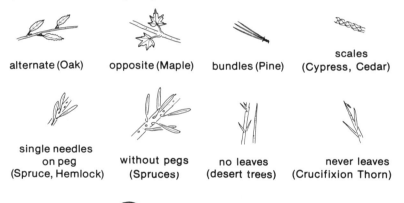

alternate (Oak)   opposite (Maple)   bundles (Pine)   scales (Cypress, Cedar)

single needles on peg (Spruce, Hemlock)   without pegs (Spruces)   no leaves (desert trees)   never leaves (Crucifixion Thorn)

If there is a ☺ it means that something about that tree is edible, the text will tell what part to eat.

If there is a ☹ watch out for the fruit or leaves—something is poisonous, or at least very bitter.

The illustrations in this book have been made almost exclusively from living trees in various parts of the west. Hope you discover them all too!

Chapter II

THE KEY TO WESTERN TREES

To use this key, look carefully at a leaf or leaves of your tree. Always try to observe the characteristics by examining more than one leaf (which doesn't mean you have to *pick* any of them—just *look* at them).

Decide: 1. What the *shape* is (long, narrow, heart-shaped, needle-like, etc.).

          2. What its usual *size* is.

          3. The *pattern* system of the veins.

          4. Whether it is a *simple* or *compound* leaf of 3 to many leaflets.

          5. How it grows on the twig—is it *alternate* or *opposite?*

          6. Try to find the *fruit* (pod, capsule, berry, cone, acorn or whatever) of the tree. Look on the ground underneath.

          7. Notice the *bark*; it may be a helpful clue.

          8. A glossary can be found on page 202.

Then: Read the first pair of clues on page 6; choose which one most fits your leaf. Look at the pictures in the margins to help you decide. Go to the clue that your chosen statement sends you to. Again, choose from that pair of clues *the* one that best fits your leaf. Sometimes there will be three clues to choose from. Be sure you read all three, then make your choice; each one will instruct you further where to go.

        Continue following clues until you find a page number given. That page will tell you about that tree or the group of trees your specimen belongs to. Sometimes a short key will be there to use if there are many kinds of trees in that group (as Pines).

Use that key the same way; it will lead you to your tree. On those pages there will be a drawing of the leaf or twig, often of the fruit, cone, or flower, and usually a silhouette that shows a typical form of that tree—how it looks from a distance, and an indication of the usual height. The description will give you more information—where it grows, how long it lives, and other interesting information.

Note: This key is designed to fit the native trees of the West. Many shrubs are included, for they often grow to tree-like proportions. There are a few non-native trees included—the Intruders. They are included in this book because they now grow so abundantly in many places, they appear "native." They are included in the key, and are grouped in Chapter V, page 190.

This key will also work with many trees that have been brought in from other places and planted in parks and along streets. Though they may not be the western species described in these pages, the key can help you find out the group or genus they belong to—i.e. whether it is a Spruce, a Fir, a Maple, or whatever.

The Key

1 a.   If the tree is a desert tree with no leaves at
           the moment . . .   **go to clue 70**

     b.   If the tree has leaves that are needle-like,
          scale-like, or broad-leafed . . .   **to clue 2**

2 a.   Leaves are needle-shape, scale-shape, or
           awl-shape, less than 5 mm wide (1/8"). It is
           a conifer . . .   **go to clue 3**

     b.   Leaves at least more than 5 mm wide (1/8")
          . . .   **go to clue 19**

a   b

3 a. Leaves are needle-like . . .   go to clue 4

  b. Leaves are scale-shaped or awl-shaped, usually overlapping closely along branch, typically much less than 5 mm wide (1/8") . . .   go to clue 13

a   b

4 a. Needle-like leaves in clusters on twig . . .   go to clue 5

  b. Needle-like leaves attached singly along twig . . .   go to clue 6

a   b

5 a. Many needles (more than 5) in clusters on short spurs. It is a Larch . . .   turn to page 52

  b. 2-5 needles in bundles, base of each bundle wrapped in papery sheath (at least young needles). It is a Pine, *Pinus* . . .   turn to page 27

a   b

6 a. Single round needle, wrapped at base by papery sheath (at least young needles). It is a Piñon Pine . . .   turn to page 41

  b. Single needle (round, flat, or angled) *not* wrapped by papery sheath . . .   go to clue 7

a   b

7   a.   Needles jointed to woody persistent pegs on twigs (old leafless twigs show these pegs) . . . **go to clue 8**

      b.   Needles (or petioles) attached *directly* to twig (or needle bases running down along twig), *not* to persis tent pegs . . .   **go to clue 9**

8   a.   Needles abruptly narrow to short petiole before joining woody peg. Apex of tree and branchlets flexible and drooping. It is a Hemlock, *Tsuga* . . .   **turn to page 58**

      b.   Needles having no petiole before joining wooden peg. Pyramidal crown; at least upper branches stiff. It is a Spruce, *Picea* . . .   **turn to page 53**

9   a.   Needles narrow at base to a very short, twisted petiole that extends down twig; fruit *not* a woody cone, but looks like a red cup-shaped berry or green olive . . .   **go to clue 10**

      b.   Needles with petiole or not; may be narrow and twisted at base or run down stem. Fruit a woody cone . . .   **go to clue 11**

10   a.   Needles stiff, more than 2.5 cm (1") long, sharp-prickled, 2 whitish lines on under-surface; olive-like fruit. It is a California Nutmeg, *Torreyana* . . .   turn to page 92

      b.   Needles not sharp-prickled; cup-like fruit. It is a Western Yew, *Taxus* . . .   turn to page 92

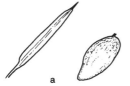 

11   a.   Needles attached by circular base, leaving round scars the size of a common pin-head on smooth twig. It is a Fir, *Abies* . . .   turn to page 64

      b.   Needles with narrow base or petiole; may leave small scar or base of leaf may extend down twig . . .   go to clue 12

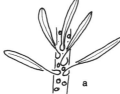 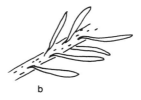

12   a.   Leaves typically not as long as 2.5 cm (1"), narrow at base and extending down twig a short ways. No bracts between cone scales. It is a Coast Redwood, *Sequoia sempervirens* . . .   turn to page 74

      b.   Leaves typically 2.5 cm (1") or longer, narrowed at base to short petiole; tiny rough leaf scars. 3-parted bracts between cone scales. It is a Douglas Fir, *Pseudotsuga* . . .   turn to page 61

 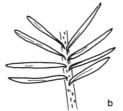 

13 a. Crush a twig; if it smells pitchy or resinous
           . . .   go to clue 14

      b. Crush a twig; doesn't smell pitchy or
          resinous, and scale-like leaves are arranged
          alternately along a tough, fine stem. It is a
          Tamarix, an Intruder . . .   turn to page 196

14 a. Leaves small, awl-shaped, overlapping
           around twig in spirals (not pairs or three's),
           pointed tips sticking out; cone 5-8 cm long
           with thick woody scales. Bark very thick,
           fibrous, deep cinnamon color. It is a Big-
           tree, *Sequoiadendron giganteum* . . .   turn to page 72

      b. Tiny, overlapping scale-shaped leaves ar-
          ranged opposite each other in pairs, or in
          circles of three, tightly against twig . . .   go to clue 15

   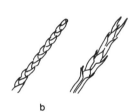

          a   b

15 a. Flat *sprays* and *branches* hanging
           gracefully—like drapes, (*twigs of Cham-
           aecyparis* may be roundish); successive pairs
           of scales differ from one another; cones
           mature in one season . . .   go to clue 16

      b. Sprays *bushy* (not flat), branchlets and twigs
          round, cord-like, or squarish; scales op-
          posite or in 3's, successive ones are alike;
          cones take 2 years to mature . . .   go to clue 18

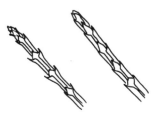

              a   b

16 a. Scale-like leaves in opposite pairs (4 scales at each node), side pair larger and folded against the flat middle pair, giving twig a "jointed" look. Woody, pendent cone of 3 pairs of oblong scales opening widely. It is Incense Cedar, *Calocedrus decurrens* . . .   turn to page 75

   b. Minute scale-like leaves in pairs (2 scales at each node), overlapping the next pair . . .   go to clue 17

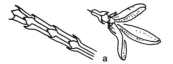 

a   b

17 a. Woody cone of 4-6 pairs of oblong, overlapping scales; cone turned back above spray. It is a Western Red Cedar, *Thuja plicata* . . .   turn to page 76

   b. Small round woody cone looking like a small Cypress cone, maturing in one year, few seeds. It is *Chamaecyparis*. . .   turn to page 81

a   b

18 a. Fruit a round, woody cone of a few closely-fitted, shield-shaped thick scales, many seeds; takes 2 years to mature. It is *Cupressus* . . .   turn to page 78

   b. Fruit a small berry, often covered by a whitish "bloom"; tips of scales project through skin. It is *Juniperus* . . .   turn to page 84

                              b

a   b

19 a. Leaves large (30-180 cm), fan-like or sword-like, crowded at top of trunk or ends of thick branches . . .   go to clue 20

   b. Leaves not fan-shape or sword-shape, usually not more than 30 cm long . . .   go to clue 21

20 a. Leaves large, fan-shape, crowded at top of trunk, old leaves hanging down like a thatch over trunk. It is a California Palm . . . turn to page 94

b. Leaves long, sword-shape, crowded at top of thick branches. It is a Joshua Tree . . . turn to page 94

21 a. Leaves simple. Margin may be smooth, serrated, toothed, jagged or lobed. . . go to clue 22

b. Leaves compound . . . go to clue 39

a   b

22 a. Palmately veined simple leaves . . . go to clue 23

b. Pinnately veined simple leaves . . . go to clue 27

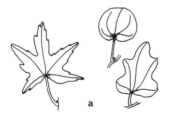
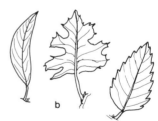

a   b

23 a. Leaves opposite each other, lobed; fruit a double samara. It is a Maple, *Acer* . . . turn to page 169

b. Leaves alternate . . . go to clue 24

a   b

24
a. Leaves lobed . . .   go to clue 25

b. Leaves not lobed . . .   go to clue 26

25
a. Large leaves deeply 5-lobed and toothed. It is a Sycamore, *Platanus* . . .   turn to page 146

b. Small leaves 2-5 cm wide, 3-lobed, "sand-grainy" or hairy. It is Fremontia, *Fremontodendron californicum* . . .   turn to page 167

26
a. Leaves almost round but with heart-shaped base; deciduous. It is Redbud, *Cercis occidentalis* . . .   turn to page 165

b. Leaves oval; evergreen. It is Wild Lilac, *Ceanothus* . . .   turn to page 178

27
a. Simple leaves with smooth, entire margins, lacking any serrations . . .   go to clue 28

b. Simple leaves with serrated, toothed, spiny or lobed margins, including minutely serrated, gland-tipped, or somewhat irregular . . .   go to clue 57

28 a. Leaves opposite . . .   go to clue 56

b. Leaves alternate, never really opposite . . .   go to clue 29

29 a. Leaves very pungent, suggesting some herb
or medicine when crushed; evergreen . . .   go to clue 30

b. Leaves not pungent . . .   go to clue 31

30 a. Long bluish-green leaves, gradually tapering
to sharp tip; bark peeling in long strips, leaving tree smooth. It is Eucalyptus, an Intru-
der . . .   turn to page 190

b. Leaves dark green, bark thin, gray and scaly.
It is California Bay, (Oregon Myrtle),
Umbellularia californica . . .   turn to page 145

31 a. Leaves very long (up to 15 cm) and very
narrow (1 cm), a desert tree with long skinny
seed pods. It is Desert Willow, *Chilopsis
linearis* . . .   turn to page 168

b. Leaves not extremely long and narrow . . .   go to clue 32

32 a. Leaves evergreen, usually thick and leathery
. . .   go to clue 33

b. Leaves not evergreen . . .   go to clue 37

33 a. Tree or large shrub with satiny-smooth terra cotta red bark or deep red-brown or purplish smooth bark . . . go to clue 34

b. Trees do not have smooth red bark . . . go to clue 35

34 a. Trees with terra cotta red bark (except at base of old trees); leaves satiny-smooth; glossy green upper surface of leaves, dull on lower; 7-14 cm long. It is Madrone, *Arbutus menziesii* . . . turn to page 181

b. Bark smooth, polished red-brown or purplish; small, many-trunked tree or large shrub; leaves 2.5-4 cm long. It is a Manzanita, *Arctostaphylos* . . . turn to page 183

35 a. Oak trees—fruit an acorn. Look for acorns or acorn cups either on or under tree. Oaks may have variously margined leaves—some can be very smooth-edged while other leaves on same branch or tree may be quite toothed. Older branches and mature trees tend to have leaves with smooth margins. It is an Oak, *Quercus* . . . turn to page 122

b. Not oak tree; does not produce acorns, but may have fuzzy-tailed seeds, nuts in a chestnut-like bur, or capsule with small seeds . . . go to clue 36

35   36

a   b   a   b

36 a. Tree or shrub with thick bark, dark green leaves that are golden underneath, bur-like coverings on small nut. It is Chinquapin, *Castanopsis chrysophylla* . . . turn to page 120

b. Angular, short-branched, stiff, smallish tree with small leaves, edges rolled under; fruit a fuzzy-tailed achene. It is Mountain Mahogany, *Cercocarpus ledifolius* . . . turn to page 149

37 a. Leaves very tiny (less than 2 cm), present only after rainy season, (look under trees for fallen leaves). A desert tree with angular branches ending in a spine. Flowers, when present, deep blue, pea-like. It is Desert Smoke Tree, *Dalea spinosa* . . . turn to page 161

b. Leaves larger; truly deciduous (dropping leaves only in the fall); tree not spiny . . . go to clue 38

38 a. Leaves "sandpapery," very noticeable net veins; leaves usually lop-sided at base. It is Hackberry, *Celtis reticulata* . . . turn to page 144

b. Leaves not sandpapery; green above, grayish below; stipules often on twiglet. Leaves at least twice as long as wide; buds are "pussies," developing into hanging catkins; small cottony seeds. It is a Willow, *Salix* . . . turn to page 108

 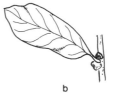

39 a. Leaves palmately compound, 5 or more leaflets. It is Buckeye, *Aesculus californica* . . . turn to page 175

b. Leaves pinnately (or double-pinnately) compound, 3 to many leaflets . . . go to clue 40

40 a. Twigs, branchlets or branches spiny; spines may be single, paired, or in 3's, or the twigs themselves taper to spiny ends . . . go to clue 41

b. No spines . . . go to clue 49

41 a. Twigs end in sharp, tapered spines; no spines along twig; leaflets (pinnules) very tiny; trunk and branches yellow-green. It is Yellow Palo Verde, *Cercidium microphyllum* . . . turn to page 159

b. Spines scattered or at regular intervals along twigs, branchlets, or branches . . . go to clue 42

42 a. Spines in pairs or in 3's . . . go to clue 43

b. Spines single . . . go to clue 47

43 a. Spines grouped in 3's; stem zigs at each thorn node. It is Horse-bean, *Parkinsonia aculeata* . . . turn to page 160

b. Spines in pairs . . . go to clue 44

44 a. Compound leaf has odd number of leaflets (so there is an end leaflet); leaflets at least as big as a thumbnail; spines dark-colored; hairy stems. It is New Mexican Locust, *Robinia neo-mexicana* . . .   turn to page 194

b. Compound leaf has even number of leaflets or pinnules (they are in pairs, so none at tip); leaflets or pinnules small; spines light color . . .   go to clue 45

a   b

45 a. Leaves evergreen, tree always appearing gray-green; wood very heavy; base of trunk peeling and scaly; fruit a few-seeded lumpy pod. It is Ironwood, *Olneya tesota* . . .   turn to page 162

b. Leaves not evergreen; tree not gray-green . . .   go to clue 46

46 a. Double-pinnately compound leaves of many small pairs of pinnules; pod hangs long— lumpy when mature. It is Honey Mesquite, *Prosopis juliflora* . . .   turn to page 163

b. Double-pinnately compound leaves usually of only 3 or 4 pairs of small pinnules; pods twist into tight spring-like coils. It is Screw-bean Mesquite, *Prosopis pubescens* . . .   turn to page 164

a   b

47 a. Spines curved or hooked. It is Catclaw, *Acacia greggii* . . .   turn to page 157

b. Spines straight, not curved . . .   go to clue 48

48 a. Usually only 2-3 pairs tiny pinnules in each compound leaf. It is Blue Palo Verde, *Cercidium floridum* ...   turn to page 158

b. 7-9 pairs, (or an odd total number) of leaflets, many as big as a person's thumb. Stipules may be spiny. It is a Locust, *Robinia pseudoacacia* ...   turn to page 194

a   b

49 a. Opposite compound leaves, usually with 3-9 leaflets (examine several sets); single-leaf ash may have 1-5 leaflets—but whatever number, leaves are opposite ...   go to clue 50

b. Alternate compound leaves, usually of 7-25 leaflets (Hoptree only has 3) ...   go to clue 51

50 a. Most of the leaves have just 3 leaflets, deeply toothed; fruit a double samara. It is a Maple, *Acer* ...   turn to page 169

b. Usually 5-7 serrate-edged leaflets; tiny whitish flowers; clusters of berries; usually small trees. It is an Elderberry, *Sambucus* ...   turn to page 186

c. 3-7 smooth or finely serrate-edged leaflets; fruit a cluster of dry single samaras. It is an Ash, *Fraxinus* ...   turn to page 184

a   b   c

51 a. Leaves double-pinnately compound with many tiny pinnules and several pinna. It is a Black Acacia, an Intruder . . . turn to page 195

b. Leaves pinnately compound . . . go to clue 52

a   b

52 a. Aromatic compound leaves; fruit a dry pinkish berry. It is a Pepper Tree, an Intruder . . . turn to page 192

b. Leaves not aromatic . . . go to clue 53

53 a. Leaflet margin entire, or with only a notch or two near base . . . go to clue 54

b. Leaflet margin serrated . . . go to clue 55

a   b

54 a. 3 leaflets; bright green, almost as broad as long. It is a Hoptree, *Ptelea augustifolia* . . . turn to page 189

b. 8-18 leaflets, no notch near base; fruit a transparent berry. It is Western Soapberry, *Sapindus drummondii* . . . turn to page 176

c. 11-25 sharply pointed leaflets with notch near base; long leaf. It is Ailanthus, an Intruder . . . turn to page 192

a   b   c

55 a. Regularly and noticeably serrated leaflets; small tree; cluster of bright orange-red berries. It is Mountain Ash, *Sorbus sitchensis* . . .   turn to page 156

   b. Finely serrated leaflets, medium sized to large tree; hard nut; dark, deeply furrowed bark. It is a Black Walnut, *Juglans* . . .   turn to page 197

a   b

56 a. Simple, opposite leaves, thin with noticeable veins; large white flower and tight head of red berries, found in cool woods. It is Dogwood, *Cornus nuttallii* . . .   turn to page 179

   b. Simple opposite leaves, with thick, leathery, undulating irregular margin; long tassel of flowers and later of grayish seed capsules. Small tree in chaparral. It is Silk-tassel Tree, *Garrya elliptica* . . .   turn to page 180

   c. Simple, leathery, almost round, opposite leaf; fruit a single dry samara in clusters. (Compound leaves with 2-5 leaflets may be on same branch or tree). It is a Single-leaf Ash, *Fraxinus anomala* . . .   turn to page 186

a   b   c

57 a. Simple leaves with serrated, including finely serrated, spiny, or toothed margins. *Not* jagged or lobed . . .   to go clue 58

   b. Simple leaves with lobed or jagged margins which may be bristle-tipped . . .   go to clue 68

a   b

58 a.   Leaves evergreen; thick, leathery, or stiff.
            Margin serrated, toothed, or spiny . . .   go to clue 59

      b.   Leaves deciduous; margin may be toothed or
            bristly, but *not* spiny . . .   go to clue 62

59 a.   Leaves narrow; margin more or less
            small-toothed; long-lasting small, hard,
            dark, bumpy berries. Younger leaves aro-
            matic if crushed. Small bushy trees near
            coast. It is Wax Myrtle, *Myrica californica*
            . . .   turn to page 99

      b.   Young leaves not aromatic; fruit various;
            leaves not narrow . . .   go to clue 60

60 a.   Shiny, holly-like leaves; underside shiny
            yellow-green; leaf often quite concave.
            Cherry-like flowers and fruits. It is Holly-
            leaf Cherry, *Prunus ilicifolia* . . .   turn to page 152

      b.   Leaves not holly-like (or if so, then not shiny
            or yellow-green underneath) . . .   go to clue 61

61 a.   Flowers inconspicuous; fruit an acorn (look
            on and under tree to find acorns or their
            cups). It is an Oak, *Quercus* . . .   turn to page 122

      b.   Fruit a berry; white flowers in clusters; leaf
            fairly large (5-10 cm) and thick, toothed all
            along the margin. It is a Toyon, *Heteromeles
            arbutifolia* . . .   turn to page 149

      c.   Fruit with a long fuzzy tail; leaf small,
            toothed from middle to tip. It is Mountain
            Mahogany, *Cercocarpus* . . .   turn to page 149

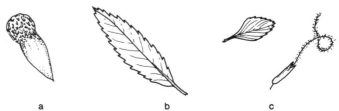

a   b   c

62 a. Deciduous leaves, long and narrow (often 4 times as long as wide). Flower buds are "pussies," opening into catkins; only 1 scale as a cap covering leaf buds; stipules present, but may fall early. It is a Willow, *Salix* . . . turn to page 108

b. Deciduous leaves not 4 times as long as wide: leaf buds with no scales or many scales . . . go to clue 63

a   b

63 a. Crushed leaves with acrid or bitter almond odor; leaves cherry- or apple-like, often with beady glands along margin or at base of blade. Cherry- or plum-like flowers and fruit. It is a *Prunus* . . . turn to page 152

b. Leaves and fruit not cherry- or plum-like; crushed leaves not like bitter almond . . . go to clue 64

a   b

64 a. Leaves with conspicuously parallel side veins that reach the margin. Fruit a woody or papery "cone" (immature or mature cones almost always can be found); leaves sharply toothed . . . go to clue 65

b. Leaves with conspicuously parallel side veins that may reach margin or curve abruptly just before margin, but *no* woody or papery "cones." . . . go to clue 66

c. Leaves with irregularly branched side veins; fruit not a papery or woody "cone" . . . go to clue 67

a   b   c

65 a. Leaves mostly on short side branchlets; woody "cones" in clusters which persist on tree for some time—look under tree too. It is an Alder, *Alnus* . . .   **turn to page 116**

    b. Leaves mostly on long branchlets (not short stubby branchlets); "cones" papery—immature ones can be seen often on tree— mature "cones" fall apart when seeds ripen. It is a Birch, *Betula* . . .   **turn to page 114**

66 a. Finely serrated, fairly large leaves near ends of branches; dark green above, underside yellow-green with hairy veins. It is Cascara Sagrada, *Rhamnus purshiana* . . .   **turn to page 177**

    b. Serrations only near tip of small leaves; shrub or small tree; dark, dryish berries. It is Service Berry, *Amelanchier alnifolia* . . .   **turn to page 150**

67 a. Stout thorns, leaf irregularly serrated; flower like a small rose. It is Black Haw, *Crataegus douglasii* . . .   **turn to page 151**

    b. No thorns; roundish, triangular or longer leaves; resinous leaf buds with many scales; flowers in catkins, tiny cottony seeds; petioles of some are flattened so leaves quiver. It is a Poplar, *Populus* . . .   **turn to page 100**

    a   b

68 a. Simple leaves with lobed or jagged margins which may be bristly (elongations of the veins and edges make the bristles); fruit an acorn; deciduous. It is an Oak, *Quercus* . . . **turn to page 122**

    b. Simple, sandpapery leaves, various lobed (at least some leaves lobed); fruit not an acorn; deciduous or evergreen . . .   **go to clue 69**

    a   b

69 a. Leaves thick, smooth margined, variously lobed, often some leaves pinnately veined, some palmately veined, sandpapery surfaces, large bright yellow flowers; evergreen. It is Fremontia, *Fremontodendron californicum* ...   turn to page 167

b. Leaves serrated, one or two-lobed (some may not be lobed), sandpapery surface; fruit a berry. It is Texas Mulbury, *Morus microphylla* ...   turn to page 188

a   b

70 a. Leafless twigs taper to spine tip ...   go to clue 71

b. Leafless twigs have spines along stem at old leaf nodes. It is Blue Palo Verde, *Cercidium floridum* ...   turn to page 158

a   b

71 a. Tree with smooth, yellow-green bark all over. It is Yellow Palo Verde, *Cercidium microphyllum* ...   turn to page 159

b. Tree is gray-green all over; brown dots on twigs. It is a Smoke Tree, *Dalea spinosa* ...   turn to page 161

c. Base of tree trunk rough, twigs flexible and green; shaggy-looking tree of upward-pointing twigs with small, dark, oval, persistent capsules. It is a Crucifixion Thorn, *Canotia holacantha* ...   turn to page 166

a   b   c

Chapter III

CONIFERS

PINES

Pines are probably the best known group of conifers. They all have evergreen, needle-shaped leaves arranged in bundles, with a membranous or papery sheath around the base of each bundle. There may be 5, 4, 3, 2, or 1 needle in the bundle, depending on the species of pine. Even when there is only one needle, there is a membranous wrapping around the needle base. Needles of some pine species loose most of this wrapping after the second or third year on the trees, but they are still held in a group or bundle. Some species have quite a wide band of this papery sheath. It is always wise to count the needles in several bundles on the tree to determine the number average within the bundles, for occasionally the number may vary.

The needles are spirally arranged on the twig and stay on the tree for many years—some species retain any one year's needles for twelve or more years.

Many pines show one to several rows of white dots down the needle length (best seen under a magnifier). These are rows of stomates, the breathing pores of leaves. They may make the leaf appear whitish or grayish.

Pines are mainly tall, conical trees, but some alpine or desert forms are often dwarfed, stunted, or twisted. The mature bark is always scaly, or fissured, or both.

The male flowers are tiny cones of many overlapping stamens, falling as soon as the pollen is shed. The female flower develops into a woody cone made of many overlapping scales, spirally arranged. Two seeds, usually with wings, develop on the upper surface of each cone scale. The cone matures at the end of the second or third season; it may fall as soon as the seeds drop, or it may hang on for months or even years. Some cones do not open unless they are broken off or are heated (as in a forest fire).

The oldest-known living tree is a pine—the Bristlecone Pine in the high mountains of southern California, Nevada, Utah, Colorado, and Arizona. In fact, it is the oldest known living *anything*—almost 5,000 years old.

The west is an area where pines are exceptionally abundant; of the 90 species of pines in the world, 19 of them are found in the Western states. Of these 19 species, 4 of them are found *only* in California. These pines are Monterey *P. radiata*, Digger *P. sabiniana*, Torrey *P. torreyana*, and Foxtail *P. balfouriana*. The diversity of habitats in the West—high mountains, desert areas, seacoast, and rain forest areas—is, of course, responsible for this variety.

Key to Species of Pines

1
a. Needles in bundles of 5 . . . go to #2

b. Needles not in bundles of 5 . . . go to #7

2
a. Needles stiff and short (2-7 cm long) . . . go to #3

b. Needles stout and long (20-30 cm long)—
Torrey Pine, *Pinus torreyana* . . . turn to page 38

c. Needles slender, 5-10 cm long . . . go to #6

3
a. Needles *very* short (2-2.5 cm), crowded; cone 5-15 cm long—Foxtail Pine, *Pinus balfouriana* . . . turn to page 37

b. Needles short, 2.5-7 cm long . . . go to #4

4
a. Needles 2.5-4 cm, curved, 3-angled, pitchy; timberline tree of high desert to Rocky Mountain; cone with slender out-pointing prickle—Bristlecone Pine, *Pinus aristata* . . . turn to page 35

b. Needles 2.5-7; cone with thickened scale tip, no prickle . . . go to #5

5 a.   Twigs thinner than a pencil; cone 8-20 cm, open when mature; mature bark with squarish, flaky plates—Limber Pine, *Pinus flexilus* . . . turn to page 33

     b.   Twigs stout, thicker than a pencil; thick cone 2.5-7.5 cm, thick scales; mature cone stays closed; mature bark thin and scaly—White Bark-Pine, *Pinus albicaulis* . . . turn to page 34

6 a.   Needles "soft," flexible and blunt; slender cone 12-23 cm long, usually curved; bark cinnamon in color, squarish flakes— Western White Pine, *Pinus monticola* . . . turn to page 30

     b.   Needles somewhat stiff, sharp-pointed; long cone 30-60 cm hanging at branch-ends; reddish bark with deep furrows and irregular scaly plates—Sugar Pine, *Pinus lambertiana* . . . turn to page 31

7 a.   Needles in bundles of four—4-needle Piñon, *Pinus quadrifolia* . . . turn to page 39

     b.   Needles in bundles of 3 or less . . . go to #8

8 a.   Needles in bundles of 3 . . . go to #9

     b.   Needles in bundles of less than 3 . . . go to #14

9 a.   Needles long (15-36 cm), gray-green or blue-green; heavy cone with thickened scale tips ending in stout spurs . . . go to #10

     b.   Needles shorter, cone may have prickle or thickened scale tips, but no stout spur . . . go to #11

10 a.   Foliage dense, needles 15-30 cm long, heavy cone, 1½ or twice as long as wide—Coulter Pine, *Pinus coulteri* . . . turn to page 46

     b.   Foliage sparse, long drooping needles, tree trunks usually forking; heavy cones, about as wide as long—Digger Pine, *Pinus sabiniana* . . . turn to page 45

11 a.   Needles usually 8-17 cm long; main branches
             and tree trunk encircled by closed cones of
             past years; solid, lop-sided cones . . .   go to #12

        b.   Needles 10-25 cm long; cones near ends of
             branches, falling soon after ripe . . .   go to #13

12 a.   Needles deep green (sometimes 2 needles to
             bundles); foliage dense; bark very dark char-
             coal in color; cone persistent for few years,
             no stalk—Monterey Pine, *Pinus radiata* . . . turn to page 47

        b.   Needles pale green, foliage sparse; branches
             slender, tip upturned; bark brown-gray;
             cone persistent for many years, with a
             stalk—Knobcone Pine, *Pinus attenuata* . . . turn to page 48

13 a.   Needles shining yellow-green; cones 7-15 cm,
             pricking hand when grabbed, bark flakes
             yellow on inside—Yellow Pine, *Pinus pon-
             derosa* . . .   turn to page 42

        b.   Needles deep green or blue-green; cones
             15-30 cm, prickles incurved and so don't
             prickle; bark flakes gray inside—Jeffrey
             Pine, *Pinus jeffreyi* . . .   turn to page 43

14 a.   One round needle in sheath; chunky
             cone—One-leaf Piñon Pine, *Pinus mono-
             phyllum* . . .   turn to page 41

        b.   Two needles in bundles . . .   go to #15

15 a.   Crowded, stiff needles, 10-15 cm long—
             Bishop Pine, *Pinus muricata* . . .   turn to page 51

        b.   Needles only 3-6 cm long . . .   go to #16

16 a.   Stiff incurving needles, gray-green or
             yellow-green; inner surface with white stom-
             ate bands; squat small cone, no prickle—
             Colorado Piñon, *Pinus edulis* . . .   turn to page 40

        b.   Needles may twist, but not incurved; deep
             green; cone with slender prickle . . .   go to #17

17 a.   Small, often twisted tree growing near sea
level—Beach Pine, *Pinus contorta* . . .   turn to page 50

      b.   Straight, tall tree, found inland, above 3,000
feet—Lodgepole Pine, *Pinus murrayana* . . . turn to page 49

WESTERN WHITE PINE
(Idaho Pine, Little Sugar, Silver Pine)
Pinus monticola

Western White Pine grows abundantly and is characteristic of the middle and upper slopes of mountains. They are found from southern British Columbia eastward through Idaho and western Montana, and south through Washington (Olympics and Cascades), Oregon (in the Cascades, Blue, and Warner Mountains), and into the northern Coast Ranges of California and through the Sierra Nevada.

Western White Pine is usually very regular in crowded forest conditions—conical, fairly tall—30-60 meters (90-180'), with all branches short. If in an open area, the tree tends to be shorter and very irregularly branched, with a few very long branches extending far beyond the others.

The branchlets are comparatively thick, the mature bark about 4 cm thick (1½"), and varies considerably. It may be cinnamon-tan in color, broken into somewhat irregular squarish plates with thin, tightly-attached scales. In other situations, it tends to be dark grayish and grooved. Young trees and branches are smooth and silvery-gray.

The blue-green needles are in 5's; they are slender, 5-10 cm long (2-4"), and tend to give the tree a "soft" appearance from a distance because of their abundance and thinness—especially as compared to the Lodgepole Pine which has short, thick needles and is often found growing side by side with the Western White Pine. The needles of the Western White Pine are blunt—unlike Sugar Pine needles which they resemble otherwise.

The cone is light weight, fairly long—15-30 cm (6-12")—with a rounded-tip, and thin scales somewhat resembling a small Sugar Pine cone. The cones have a long stalk and hang in clusters at branch ends. The cones are very slender when closed, curved towards the tip, and can be dark purple or dark green when young.

The inside of the scales is deep red, the tips a warm tan, as are the twin areas on each scale where the seed and its wing were held—all making a very striking, colorful pattern. The seeds are small with tiny black spots and thin wings.

This is a common, excellent softwood lumber tree, often called merely "White Pine" or "Idaho Pine" by lumbermen. It is used principally where straight grain and light weight are needed, and to make wooden matches. It is very similar to Eastern White Pine. Usually lives for 200-500 years, though is very susceptible to pine blister rust disease. May be found from 2,000 feet elevation in the north to 10,000 feet in southern range, with Red Fir, Lodgepole, and Jeffrey.

SUGAR PINE
Pinus lambertiana

Sugar Pine is a beautiful, big, forest tree. It is the largest of the pines, and is found in Oregon and California. It is especially known because of its very long, big cones which hang singly or in groups of 2 or 3 from the tips of long branches. Often grows to 75 meters (225') and may be as much as 4 meters (12') in diameter. The trunk is almost always very straight with little taper until near the top.

The branches tend to be fairly sparse in mature trees, with a few extra long ones, and all extending at right angles to the trunk.

The gray-brown bark is deeply furrowed, then fissured horizontally at irregular intervals to produce large long plates. The surface is loose-flaky, and if these have been peeled off by the wind, etc. those areas will be red-brown. The bark of branches and young trunks are a smooth, thin, dark gray.

There are five stiff, sharp-pointed needles to the bundle, but be sure to count several bundles, especially if examining new growth, for twigs sometimes have some bundles of 3 and even some of 4 needles, but the majority will be five. The membranous wrapping may be very short or almost gone on the old needles. The needles vary from 7-10 cm long (3-4'').

The cones are exceptionally long and beautiful though not heavy or massive. They hang from stalks 5-8 cm long (2-3''). The cone is much the same diameter over its whole length and may be 25-40 cm long (10-24''), or up to 55 cm. The scale tips are shiny, pale brown on the inside, and very broad. The cones mature in the autumn of the second year, drop their seeds in October but remain on the tree till the next summer, so there are cones noticeable on the tree almost year-round, though they are not always full-grown.

Sugar Pines are found on mountain slopes and ridges of the Coast Ranges and Cascades of Oregon, south through the northern Coast Ranges of California down to Baja California. They are especially abundant in the Sierra Nevada. Sugar Pines are one of the main forest trees of the western slope of the Sierra Nevada along with Yellow Pine, Jeffrey Pine and Giant Sequoia. In Oregon it is found near the coast at an elevation of 1,000 to 5,000 feet on the east side of the Cascades. In California it is usually found between 3,500 and 7,500 feet elevation.

LIMBER PINE
Pinus flexilis

Limber Pine is well-named, for this tree can withstand strong winds by bending before them, and its thinner branches are so flexible they can be tied in knots without breaking. Truly a tree to withstand the sweeping cold winds and short growing seasons of high, dry, mountain areas.

The needles (5 to a bundle) are thick, stiff, and vary in length from 2.5-7 cm (1-1½''), densely covering the branch ends like bottlebrushes. The dark brown or cinnamon bark on mature trees is at least 2.5 cm thick, broken into square, flaky plates. Young trees have smooth, pewter-colored bark. The purplish slender cones

(5-12 cm) are produced in groups which stick out horizontally or slightly downward. When mature, the open scales show their pale red inner surfaces with the distinctly thickened scale tips turning light golden brown—this is an identifying characteristic. The cones have usually fallen by early winter.

This pine grows best on dry, gravelly, or rocky spots—mineral soils with scant humus. It is found high in the western mountains—from the eastern side of the Rockies, north and west to Alberta, south through the high mountains of Nevada and westward to both eastern and southern California. It is found at elevations from 7,500–11,000 feet. It tends to grow a thick but short trunk with side branches often almost as big as the main trunk.

Limber Pine is usually found clinging to windswept slopes or ridges. In such a situation, the lead branches tend to be found mainly on one side (even if they originate from other side). The crown itself may be swept sideways (or broken), and the upper branches often take over as the leaders. Big right-angle branches may develop at the expense of the main trunk.

Limber Pine is occasionally found in forest situations with Lodgepole Pine, Black Hemlock, and Red Fir, and then it usually grows quite straight with regular branching. Even then Limber Pine retains the typical tight clusters of needles at the tips of the four to eight lead branches. This gives the branches a definite dark green triangular tip silhouette. It grows far more abundantly in the Rocky Mountains than in the Sierra Nevada, for it definitely prefers more arid conditions. In the Sierra Nevada it is found on the drier eastern side, mainly south from Mono Pass.

WHITE BARK PINE
Pinus albicaulis

White Bark Pine is a timberline tree, common on summits of mountains of the northwest, but not on the coastal mountains.

The trunk usually is twisted and crooked, often sprawling over the rocks, with a dwarf or bonzai form. It may grow to 15 meters (45'), and commonly has two or three trunks from the base. The branches are exceptionally flexible, which makes it possible to withstand the storms that sweep over them. The branches are at right angles to the trunk, but then tend to sweep up.

The bark on mature trees is thin and quite smooth, with whitish or brownish scales, but definitely giving the appearance of whiteness even on mature trees. Other pines, such as *P. flexilis* and *P. aristata* have whitish bark, but only on young trees. The branchlets are definitely stout, twigs likewise.

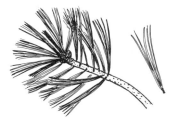 

The dark green needles are stiff, 2.5-6 cm long (1-2½''), and thickly arranged on the fat twig. They last for seven to eight years. The male and female flowers are brightly colored, the young cones stand erect the first year, then in the second year turn sideways. The smallish cones have very thick scales, coming to a snout. The scales are quite triangular in shape and thick, then thinning and narrowing down to the bent tip. At the thick middle portion they are closely appressed, with a ridge on the lower scale that fits tightly against the edge of the one above, the bent tip projecting. The cones are quite purple when ripe, but they do not open. They dry to yellowish-brown, staying closed. The seeds are large and sweet, but only the breaking of the cone releases them—which small mammals and some birds do very well. The cones may be almost as wide as long (3-7.5 cm or 1½-3'').

White Bark Pine grows from British Columbia and Alberta, south through Washington (but not in the Olympics) where it is found between 5,500 and 9,300 feet, east through Idaho and Montana where it is found between 5,000 and 10,000 feet, south through the northern parts of Wyoming and Utah, and also in California's Sierra Nevada range between elevations of 7,000 and 11,000.

BRISTLECONE PINE
Pinus aristata

The Bristlecone Pine is the oldest known living thing—centuries older than the Giant Sequoia, which for a while was given that title. Living Sequoias are probably only 2,000 to 2,700 years old, and even tremendous stumps of ones long dead do not have the age of the living Bristlecones! The oldest Bristlecone yet found is 4,600 (forty-six *hundred*) years old! Bristlecone is an alpine tree growing between 7,500 and 11,500 feet elevation. It grows at times 7-15 meters tall (20-45'), but in high, windswept, deep snow ridges it may be much dwarfed.

The trunk is usually short, with a wide, heavy, bushy crown. The lower branches tend to be short and droopy, the upper ones longer

and irregular. Branches and the trunks of young trees are smooth, almost chalky white, while mature trunks are reddish or dark brown with irregular shallow fissures and flat scaly ridges.

The deep green needles, in bundles of five, are curved and seem to be brushed forward and clustered at the ends of the stout branches. They extend down the branch some distance so it looks like a bushy tail. The needles are 3-angled and fairly thin and whitish on their inner surface. They frequently seem to have flecks of white pitch on them and the branches seem to have a fair amount of pitch on them, too. The needles last for many years, probably 12-15, which helps to produce the thick-looking foliage. More importantly, this helps the tree stay alive over years of poorer conditions.

The cone takes two years to mature. It is a deep chocolate color, tinged with purple. Each scale has a thickened end with a small beak and a curved, fragile prickle which is often broken off.

Bristlecones usually grow as scattered trees or in small groups. It is found mainly by itself, but may be with Limber Pine, on high barren ridges, ledges, and high peaks, mainly on the south slopes, in thin rocky soil, which is often volcanic. There is little other plant growth around—only these tough oldsters seem able to take the stark conditions of their high homes.

Found in isolated areas of Colorado, Utah, central and southern Nevada, northern Arizona, New Mexico, and the high desert mountains of southeastern California—the Inyo, Panamint, and White Mountains. They are not found in the Sierra Nevada. The Ancient Bristlecone Pine Forest—a part of the Inyo National Forest in the White Mountains, is an area where these are particularly marvelous and can be visited.

FOXTAIL PINE
Pinus balfouriana

The crowded, thick, stiff needles at the branch tips give this pine its common name. It is a timberline tree and many people confuse this with the Bristlecone. The needles of the Foxtail Pine are shorter, thicker and stiff while needles of the Bristlecone tend to be longer than 2.5 cm (1'') and fairly thin. Also, *P. balfouriana* is found only in the Sierra Nevada and Coast Ranges of California while *P. aristata* is a high mountain tree of desert regions.

The crown is bushy but narrow with short spreading branches which are very irregular in length. This is an amazing silhouette for a timberline tree, for at those altitudes trees are often gnarled and stunted. The top branches of the Foxtail Pine often die off, but it stays upright and the lower branches will be thick with foliage.

The stout, stiff needles are blue-green on the outer surface, the lower or inner surface whitish with many rows of stomates. They stay on for 8-12 years or more, which helps to produce such thick foliage (and helps this timberline tree in its short growing season).

The dark red-brown cone is 3.5-7.5 cm long (2-5''), the thick
scale tips ridged and with a minute prickle very different from the
Bristlecone. (This may be rubbed off old cones.)

The Foxtail Pine is found on dry rocky slopes and ridges from
about 10,000–11,500 feet elevation in the south, and above 6,000
feet in the northern area at timberline. This is one of the four pines
only found in California. It grows in two general areas—300 miles
apart! The southern area is found mainly within the Sequoia and
King's Canyon National Parks; the second area is in the northern
Coast Ranges—the Salmon, Scott and Yolla Bolly Mountains.

TORREY PINE
(Soledad Pine)
Pinus torreyana

Torrey Pine, though rare and growing only in a very limited area
of the southern California coast may grow to be a huge tree when
planted in many large parks. It produces tremendous branches
which tend to sweep up and then out, arching. In its wind-swept
habitat, it tends to be beaten into strikingly irregular and one-sided
picturesque forms and is often only 3-6 meters tall.

The trunk frequently divides part way up. The lower trunk of
mature trees is purplish-gray, somewhat fissured and scaly. Upper

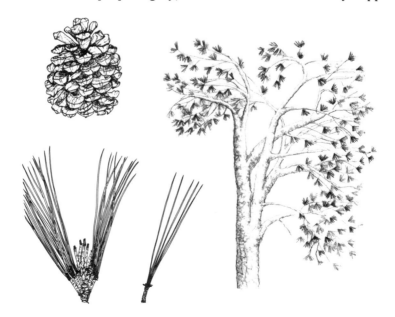

trunks and large branches are dark steel-gray, rough and scaly but not fissured. The twigs are very stout, the first two years they are green, but by third year, turn dark steel-gray.

The needles carry out these same features of bigness, they are long—20-32 cm (8-13''). They are stout and in bundles of 5. They are three-sided and have whitish stomate lines along them.

The rich, brown, ripe cones are also large—10-15 cm (4-6'') and are as wide as long, asymmetrical with the scales thickened, then tapering to a sharp bent projection not a spine.

The Torrey is one of the four pines that grow only in California—this one on a coastal island (Santa Rosa Island) and a small area in San Diego County—Del Mar.

4-NEEDLE PIÑON
(Parry Piñon)
Pinus quadrifolia

This nut pine is much like the One-leafed and the Two-leafed Piñon trees except the needles are mostly in 4's—sometimes there are needles in bundles of 3's and 5's on the same tree. Always be sure to count several bundles on any pine! Having 4 needles is unique in pines. The needles are pale blue-green on the back, the inner surface has definite white stomate rows. The needles are 3-5 cm long (1½-2''), stiff, curved, and 3-sided.

The tree is short-trunked, and many branched, forming a pyramidal silhouette when young, but becoming flat-topped as it matures. Old trees are often twisted and gnarled. The trunk is dark reddish-brown with shallow irregular grooves and tight-scaly connected ridges.

The brown cones are squat, 3.5-5 cm long, and the scale tip very thick with a rough knob. They mature in August of the second year

and the seeds are shed by mid-September. The seeds are large, edible and were an important food for Indians, as well as for birds and small mammals.

Scattered trees can be found on dry desert and mountain slopes from 2,500-5,500 feet elevation on the western edge of the Colorado Desert of southern California, southward to Baja California.

COLORADO PIÑON
(New Mexican Piñon, Two-leafed Piñon)
Pinus edulis

This is the state tree of New Mexico and grows abundantly over the hills, mesas, and low mountains. It is a short, small tree as one would expect in dry areas, with a rounded top and many branches, often from or near the base.

The stiff, incurving needles are, when new or on young trees, gray-green but older ones are dark yellow-green. The inner surface has many rows of stomates, and so appears whitish. The needles are thick and are 3-5 cm long (1½-2'').

The shiny cones usually grow singly at the branchlet ends and have far fewer scales than the One-needle Piñon, but resemble it in shape. The scales are thickened and humped at the tip, but have no spine or hook. They open widely, releasing the thin-shelled, wing-

less seeds which are edible. The bottom scales are small, don't produce seeds and remain closed.

The Colorado Piñon grows in the southern Rockies—in the Uinta Mountains, south and west to Arizona, and from southern Colorado through New Mexico and western Texas into Mexico.

PIÑON PINE
(Nut pine, One-needle Pine)
Pinus monophylla

Piñon Pine is unique in that it only has one needle to a bundle—still called a "bundle" because the bases of the young needles are enclosed with a membranous wrapping. As with other pines in this group, this wrapping drops off as the needles age. The needles are stout, cylindrical, gray-green and almost always curved. They are thickly clustered on the gray branches. Very young trees or some branches may produce leaves with two in a bundle.

The trees are generally smallish, though they may grow to 15 meters (45'), with stout, branching trunks. The crown is usually round in young trees, flat-topped as the tree ages. The branches are heavy, frequently bending downward.

The cone is chunky—larger than the needles are long, and the four-sided thick, knobby scales each hold two large very edible nuts, which unlike most pines, do not have "wings."

The Piñon Pine is a very slow-growing tree of dry rocky canyon sides, ridges and mesas, living from one hundred to more than two

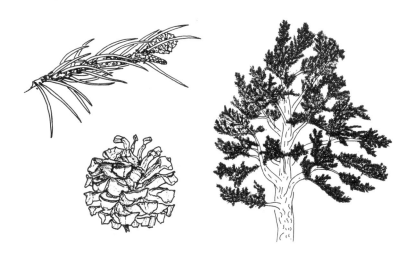

hundred years. It grows with desert junipers, but more often is found in a belt just above the junipers. It is found in the western Wasatch Mountains of Utah, on the Nevada and northern Arizona desert slopes, the east side of the Sierra Nevada (where it is the dominant tree south of Lake Tahoe), in the southern part of the west slope of the Sierra and into Baja California. It can be found in elevations from 3,500 to 9,000 feet, and will endure temperatures varying from -2° to 122° F.

YELLOW PINE
(Ponderosa Pine)
Pinus ponderosa

Yellow Pine is a beautiful, large, single-trunk tree found in every western state, including North Dakota, South Dakota, and Nebraska, though east of the Rockies the tree is often regarded as a different variety. Yellow Pine is abundant in the mountains of the west—Cascades, Sierra Nevada, Coast Ranges, Bitterroots, Rocky Mountains, Uinta Mountains, and the Ruby Range of Nevada, and is found from 200–6,000 feet elevation, depending on latitude and exposure. It is not found in the desert mountains of Nevada except in the south and east. It also grows north into British Columbia and south in both Baja California and Mexico.

The large, straight, tawny-russet trunk produces many large bent branches, each turning upward at the end. This is characteristic

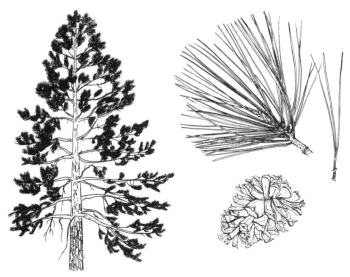

even of lower branches which may bend and twist downwards, but the tips themselves will be upturned.

The tree may grow to 40 or more meters (125'), often with practically no branches for the first 12-15 meters. The diameter averages 90-120 cm (3-4'), but larger ones are regularly found.

The rich yellow-green needles seem to reflect the sunlight in a particularly shimmering way. There are 3 needles to the bundle, usually about 15 cm (6") long, but may vary from 10-28 cm (4-11"). Each season's needles remain on the tree for 3-5 years. They grow thickly on the ends of branches; the older, bare part of each small branch is gray and thickly covered with the old leaf scars.

The thick bark of a mature tree is broken into large shield-like areas, with the surface of thinnish scales all appearing like pieces from a jigsaw puzzle which develops as the tree matures. Young trees have dark reddish-black, thinner bark that is narrowly furrowed.

The cones may be as small as 7 cm (3") or as long as 15 cm (6") and usually 3-5 cm wide (1½-2"). They mature in August of the second year and may be greenish or purplish. Most pines do not show this much variation in cone color. After the seeds are dropped (usually September), the cones start dropping and they are all off the tree by late October. Large trees often produce 1,000 cones; the ground may seem covered with cones when they have all fallen. Such a tree may produce 6 pounds of seed. The yellow-brown seeds are mottled or spotted, and the wing fairly small, as are the seeds. The ends of the cone scales become shiny red-brown as the cones mature and bend in such a way that the tip prickle sticks straight out. The cones are small enough to be hand-held, but they prickle the fingers as you close your hand around them. As someone remarked, you can recognize a cone from this species by this characteristic: if the cone prickles, it is a—"Yell -ow" Pine.

JEFFREY PINE
(Bull Pine)
Pinus jeffreyii

A marvelous big forest pine of the west coast from the Siskiyou Mountains of southern Oregon through the northern Coast Ranges of California (at almost sea level) and the Sierra Nevada to Baja California, especially large and abundant on the eastern slopes of the Sierra. It usually grows at higher elevations than the Yellow Pine, which it somewhat resembles. However, it is generally a

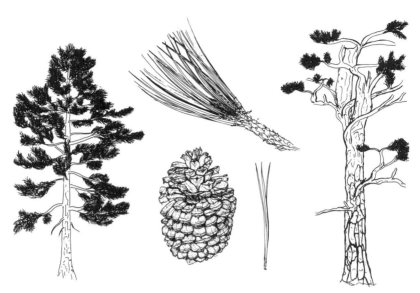

smaller tree, with bluish, deep green foliage (not yellow-green as the Yellow Pine), with bigger cones and smooth branchlets. The reddish-brown bark of Jeffrey Pine is darker and in much bigger plates and the scales are not as easily popped off. Its odor resembles vanilla or pineapple—Yellow Pine has a faint citrus-like smell at times.

It grows from 20-60 meters tall (60-180'), and to almost 2 meters in diameter. The twigs are distinctly purple when they are young. The dark bluish-green needles are in bundles of 3, quite long (12-2 cm; 5-11''), and grow very thickly along the branchlets. They live for 5-8 years, much longer than most needles, so the tree seems very dense.

The dark red-purple cones develop back from the tip of the branch. They are too big to hold in your hand comfortably (15-30 cm—6-12''). Each thick-tipped scale has a prickle, but the scale tips open so widely that the prickles are turned down and do not prick you when you handle them (as the Yellow Pine does). The dry cone is deep red-brown in color. The seeds are a mottled brown (as are Yellow Pine), but they are much bigger. It produces an abundance of seed once it matures.

The biggest and best Jeffrey Pines are found mainly above the Yellow Pine belt, in places as pure stands, but mainly found with Lodgepole Pine, Red and White Fir, Incense Cedar and Sugar Pine. It hybridizes with both Yellow Pine and Coulter Pine. It is found between 5,000 and 9,000 feet elevation.

DIGGER PINE
Pinus sabiniana

Digger Pine is the distinctive and easily recognized pine of the foothill areas of the Sierra Nevada and dry Coast Ranges in California (not in the cooler fog area of the northern Coast Ranges). Its silhouette is quickly identifiable—the trunk usually dividing into 2 or more main forks, not conical as is typical of pines. The tree appears "open" with sparse branching and foliage. The needles are in 3's, gray-green, long (20-36 cm; 8-12''), and drooping. They are not closely spaced along the branches, but are scattered except for a loose tuft at the end.

The cones are magnificent, for they are rich chocolate color, big and heavy, and each scale is elongated into a stout hook or claw pointing downwards. They tend to be almost as wide as long, and measure 16-35 cm (6-14''). They are on the end of a 2-4 cm stalk, the lower scales staying with this stalk when the cone falls. They persist on the tree for several years, slowly dropping the seeds after they mature at the end of 2 years.

Digger Pines grow scattered among other upper Sonoran trees and shrubs such as Blue Oak, Buckeye, Manzanita, and Redbud in grassy open stands usually between 50 and 2,000 feet elevation, though it is found in higher elevations farther south.

The tree grows to 13-17 meters (40-50') most often, though some grow to 30 meters. The trunk is usually .3-1.2 meters in diameter.

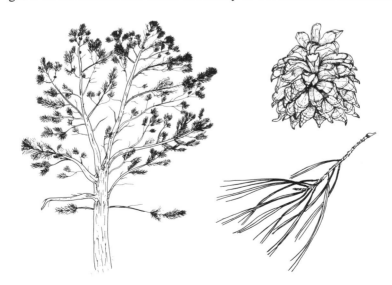

COULTER PINE
(Big Cone Pine)
Pinus coulteri

This bluish-green pine somewhat resembles the Digger Pine *(Pinus sabiniana)*, but the needles are longer, radiate from branch ends and are a deep blue-green—much less gray than those of the Digger Pine. The needles are also stiff and stout, not drooping, and are much more closely spaced so the tree appears more dense.

The cones are heavy and constructed much like those of the Digger, but more so—the thickened scale tips with a stronger hook, the cones much bigger and longer and always at least twice as long as it is wide—while Diggers are often almost as wide as they are long.

The tree grows to 25 meters (75') with a broad conical crown or, more often, quite an asymmetrical one. The bark is black-brown with scaly broad ridges and deep irregular furrows. The branchlets are rough and stout, dark orange turning to charcoal color.

The stiff needles are 15-30 cm long (6-12''). They are 3-sided and have many definite light colored stomate bands running their length. The needles stay on the tree for 3-4 years.

The light tan cones are heavy and long—25-40 cm (10-16'') with the thick scales ending in a strong incurved spur or hook. They may weight 2-4 kilos (5-9 lbs.). The cones hang on the tree for several years after the seed has fallen.

Found on dry, rocky slopes between 1,500 and 7,000 feet. It can be found from Mt. Diablo in central California, south through the

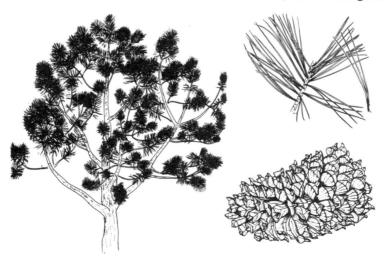

inner Coast Ranges to southern California and into Baja. It is most abundant in the San Bernardino and San Jacinto Mountains of southern California, and mainly grows with Yellow Pine or Digger Pine.

MONTEREY PINE
Pinus radiata

This pine is very restricted in its natural habitat—it is found along (but not far inland) the central California coast and its off-shore island, plus on an island off Baja California.

The Monterey Pine grows very rapidly at first. It is a regularly-branching tree, with long, actively-growing side branches and tip, producing a narrow crown. Old or mature trees usually develop an open or irregular crown with a few big branches, with the lower trunk and lower part of each branch quite bare of living foliage or side branches. Foliage will be quite dense near the ends of the living branches.

The deep green needles are in 3's (though some branches may have quite a number in bundles of 2). They are slender, but not drooping, and are 11-15 cm long (4.5-6'').

The bark of young trees or actively growing branches is dull gray, but mature trunks become reddish or very dark brown-black with narrow ridges and furrows.

The cones are heavy, 15-25 cm long, remaining on the tree for several years, tightly closed. If cut off, they will soon start to open. The scientific name for this tree is excellent, for the scales of the

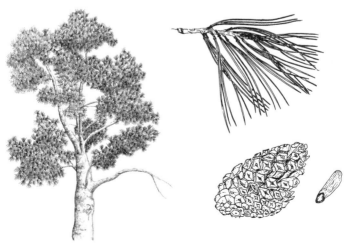

cones are so arranged that they seem to *radiate*. They are usually one-sided at the base, for they grow along the branch, not at the tip as do some pinecones, and since they stay on for years, they are pushed that way by the growing branch. Frequently there will be several at one spot, more or less encircling the branch. One of the noticeable characteristics of a mature silhouette is the cone pattern, with many on the older, lower (often dead) branches. The tips of the cone scales are thick, shiny, red-brown, with no prickle or hook; the inner surface of the scale is dark purple.

Because of its coastal habitat, it often develops marvelous, picturesque wind-swept silhouettes in maturity.

KNOBCONE PINE
Pinus attenuata (tuberculata)

Knobcone Pine is generally a fairly small tree from 8-15 meters tall (25-45'), though it may sometimes grow twice that tall. It is a fairly thin-foliaged tree and often will develop a forked trunk about midway. As it grows older, the crown becomes scraggly. The tips of the branches tend to bend upwards sharply.

The gray-green needles are in bundles of 3 and are spaced out on the branchlets, giving the tree an open thinnish silhouette.

The cones are short-stalked, usually in whorls around the trunk and the larger branches, and remain closed and on the tree for

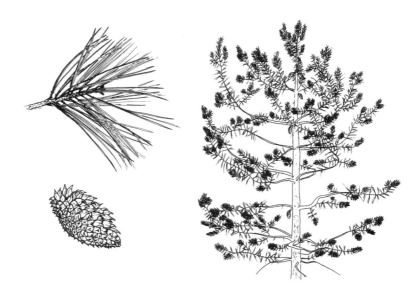

years—often for as many as thirty years! When they stay on for many years, they begin to become buried in the bark. They will not open, apparently, at least until the branch dies, which is usually not until the tree dies. But when fire sweeps through a forest and the trees are killed, the cones then open, drop their seeds and new Knobcone seedlings soon sprout. Because of this persistence, there will be a series of cones from the past many growth years still circling the trunk. They are 7.5-13 cm long (3-6''), very solid, heavy, and knobby. The cones are asymmetrical and bent downward, with the outer scales enlarged and knobby with a thick incurved prickle.

The wood is very light, weak and coarse-grained. Knobcones seem to prefer dry, exposed, rocky slopes below 4,000 feet with scattered Douglas Fir and/or chaparral. It is not abundant, growing in scattered places, from the Santa Ana Mountains of southern California, northward in various parts of the Coast Ranges, and from the Yosemite region northward in the California Sierra to southern Oregon and the Cascades.

LODGEPOLE
(Tamrac, Tamarack Pine)
Pinus murrayana

The Lodgepole Pine is most often seen growing as a crowded forest in practically pure stands. In this situation, the trees are very straight, tall, and narrow, the trunk very gradually tapering. The upper branches trend upward, middle branches horizontally, and lower branches droop, with many of the lower ones dead because

of the crowding and shading. When growing in more open areas, the trees become much larger and bigger-branched. It will range in either situation from 15-40 meters tall (45-120').

The yellow-green needles are in bundles of 2, are 3-6 cm long, fairly stout, but variable in length and width. The young needles have much membranous wrapping at the base of the bundle, while older ones have very little. The stiff, short needles help to identify the silhouette from a distance, for it gives a stiff aspect to the tree.

The bark is very characteristic and very different from most pines in that it is thin and made of close-fitting, firm, but small scales varying over the surface from yellowish to light salmon to light brown.

The cones are much like the Beach Pine, but less one-sided at the base and they tend to fall soon after dropping seed. They are small (2-5 cm), usually shorter than the needles, and with a sharp prickle on each scale. They absorb water readily when dry—after a rain in the mountains, the scales will all be bent upwards and the cone tightly closed, opening again as it dries out.

Lodgepole Pine grows in the mountains, particularly on the drier slopes, from 5,000 to 11,000 feet, often coming in quickly after a fire. Found from the southern Sierra Nevada and Baja California north to Alaska and also abundantly in the Rocky Mountains.

BEACH PINE
Pinus contorta

Beach Pine is a low, often contorted tree, with a short trunk and many stout side branches. It grows along the Pacific Coast from Alaska to northern California.

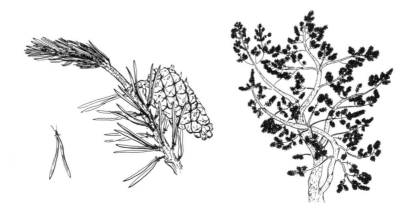

The dark green needles are short (3-5 cm), closely arranged on the branches. The young branches at first are orange, then turn to very dark brownish-black. The rich brown cones are small (2-5 cm), usually shorter than the needles, and somewhat one-sided at the base. There is a thin prickle on each cone scale. The cones grow at branch tips, often grouped, and tend to be very persistent on the tree after opening. They resemble the Lodgepole Pine cones.

BISHOP PINE
(Prickle-cone Pine)
Pinus muricata

The Bishop Pine is a small tree 15-25 meters tall (45-75'). Young trees in the open have dense pyramidal crowns and short clear trunks. Old trees have round-topped, compact crowns with the thick, spreading branches extending low to the ground, or the top may be broken off, with the remaining branches forming a flat-top silhouette. There are always many branches, frequently bent and twisted, the branchlets brownish and slender. The bark soon becomes deeply furrowed and on mature trees has dark purplish-brown scales on the ridges.

The very stiff needles are in bundles of 2 in tight clusters at the branch ends. They are dark yellow-green, 10-15 cm long (4-6'') and stay on the tree for 2-3 years. The sessile cones (attached directly at the cone base) are 5-7 cm long, asymmetrical and bent downwards,

arranged in whorls around the trunk and branches. The outer scales are thickened into knobs with a stout curved prickle. The side with the enlarged knob-like scales ends abruptly, the remainder of the scales have a sharp spine and are slightly thicker at the tip, but very much smaller. The cones are mature by August of the second year and are a shiny red-brown. Some open and drop their seeds in September and October, but many remain closed and on the tree for years. Even open ones usually do not fall until the tree dies. They

It grows abundantly near the coast of northern California from Pt. Reyes north of San Francisco to San Francisco, then in scattered groves to southern California, and also in Baja California.

LARCH
(Tamarack, Western Larch)
Larix occidentalis

Larches, along with the Dawn Redwood, are amazing conifers in that they are *not* evergreen. Each fall the Larches turn a brilliant golden yellow and then drop their needles, leaving short stout stubs on all the twigs. The needles don't persist as is characteristic of conifers, but the cones stay on the trees for years after the seeds have dropped, turning very dark—almost black—and making a very somber-looking tree during the winters. The stubs or spurs from which the many thin needles grow will show annual growth rings, and next year's needles will unfold from the bud at the tip.

Larches tend to be slender and straight, with short branches in whorls, which usually droop. In young trees, the branches may

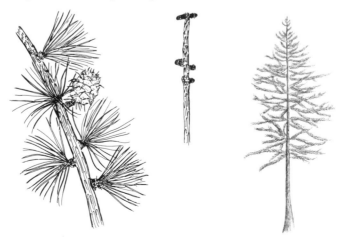

droop to the ground, but older trees lose these low branches. The bark on young trees is scaly and flakes easily, while mature trees develop deep furrows and large rough ridges in the reddish-brown thick bark.

The needles are very slender, 2.5-3.5 cm long with many (20-30) in a group growing from the dark gray stubs or spurs. Or, at the growing tip ends. the needles grow singly and spirally around the twig—a scale-like pattern persists on the stem which shows this young leaf arrangement. The needles are very light green—very different from the usual conifer colors.

The cones, when young, are purplish with long thin bracts which extend beyond the thin rounded scales. The small cones are velvety-hairy and 1.5-2.0 cm long, growing at any angle along the branchlet.

Larches are common trees mixed in with other forest trees from southeastern British Columbia, south and east through the mountains of northern Montana, Idaho, Washington and northern Oregon—especially abundant in the Bitterroot Mountains from 2,000–7,000 feet.

SPRUCE
Picea

Key To Species of Spruces

1 a.   Needles 4-sided; stomata on all sides . . .   go to #2

    b.   Needles flattened on one side, rounded on other; stomata on upper side only . . .   go to #4

2 a.   If needle is sharp and definitely prickles—Colorado Blue Spruce, *Picea pungens* . . .   turn to page 57

    b.   If needle is blunt or sharpish but doesn't prickle . . .   go to #3

3 a.   Crushed new growth with skunk-like odor; cone scale rounded, very thin; needles all around twig—White Spruce, *Picea glauca* . . .   turn to page 54

    b.   Cone scale with irregular margin and blunt; needles tend to curve up around twig— Engelmann Spruce, *Picea engelmannii* . . .   turn to page 54

4
a. Needles stiff with a small prickle; bluish-
    green—Sitka Spruce, *Picea sitchensis* . . .   turn to page 56

b. Needles flexible, blunt; shiny green—
    Weeping Spruce, *Picea breweriana* . . .   turn to page 57

WHITE SPRUCE
Picea glauca

The White Spruce is a beautiful tree, often with a spire-like tip, whorls of regular, thick branches, the lower branches first swooping down, then up. There may be numerous drooping side branchlets. If it grows in the open, it tends to keep its lower branches; in forests it will be clear of branches for 18-20 meters (48-60'). In parts of Alaska, however, it may be stunted.

The needles are four-sided and tend to be bluish-green, sometimes even appearing quite whitish. They stand out all around the twig, except near the twig tip where they all tend to turn upwards. New growth, when crushed, tends to give off a skunk-like odor.

By end of summer when the cones are ripe, they are grass-green tinged with red or rose. The seeds drop in September, and the cones then turn clay-colored and drop off the tree between then and the next spring. Cones vary in size from 2.5-6 cm (1-2½'') and the scales are very thin and flexible.

In the east, the White Spruce is extensively used for pulpwood, but in the far north, it is used for construction—an excellent wood. It is mainly a tree of the northlands—it is abundant in Yukon Territory in Alaska, in the Rocky Mountains of British Columbia and Alberta (where it grows the biggest). It also grows farther south, in Montana and Wyoming, and east through Michigan, to Maine, and is also found in South Dakota's Black Hills. The variety *albertiana* is the type found in the northern Rockies and tends to be a bigger tree.

ENGELMANN SPRUCE
Picea engelmannii

Engelmann Spruce is the tall pyramidal spruce generally found in the high mountain forests of the west. It is more abundant in the

Rocky Mountains than it is in the mountains further west. It grows to be 50 meters tall (150'), fairly slender, but with regular tiers of branches. Often it is quite dwarfed and wide-spreading at high elevations or in windswept areas. The bark is thin, a reddish-gray color with large loose scales.

The needles grow all around the twig, though the ones of the lower side twist upwards somewhat (so you see the woody twig itself from the underside while from above, you mainly see the thickly arranged soft-appearing needles). Each needle grows from a peg which remains on the twig after the leaf has dropped. Needles usually last for 7-10 years. The flexible needles are 1-2 cm long and are 4-sided, not triangular or flattened, and are the same color on all sides. When you grasp the twig, the needles are soft to the touch, not prickly.

The oblong cone is thin-scaled, with the broadest part near the middle, and gradually narrows to the squarish or slightly blunt tip. The margins are somewhat irregular or wavy. They are fairly abundant, pendant, and usually produced just on the upper half of the tree. The cones mature in one year and fall soon after dropping their seeds. When dry, the cones are a shiny tan color.

Engelmann Spruce is found abundantly in the high Rocky Mountains from British Columbia to Arizona and in the Cascades of Washington and Oregon. It grows from mid-elevations to timber line.

SITKA SPRUCE
Picea sitchensis

Sitka Spruce is a beautiful tree in the coastal forest areas of the Northwest. It can be recognized as a spruce because its needles are jointed at the base to persistent woody pegs which can be seen on twigs which have lost their needles. The needles are flattened, whitened in two bands on the upper surface, rounded and green on lower surface—thus the tree appears somewhat frosted and silvery because of these whitish stomate bands. The needles are arranged spirally all the way around the twig. Engelmann Spruce twists its needles so the spray appears semi-circular in section, while the needle arrangements of Sitka Spruce is more spherical. The needles are 1.5-2.5 cm long, somewhat flattened (not four-sided) and are pointed and sharpish.

The bark is thin, covered with lose dark red-brown scales. This is a pyramidal tree with regular, horizontal branches and may grow to 70 meters (210'), but more frequently 35 meters (100').

The cones are oval-oblong, 6-10 cm long, with the thin stiff scales rounded and slightly toothed at the tip, and with toothed, wavy edges.

The Sitka Spruce grows in very moist, even swampy places, especially in sandy soils, from Kodiak Island in Alaska to Mendocino County in northern California.

COLORADO BLUE SPRUCE
Picea pungens

The Colorado Blue Spruce, as a specimen tree in a garden or park, is well-known, for it is commonly planted all over the country, and is truly a lovely bluish-frosted color. This coloration has been achieved by carefully selecting seedlings and propagating those with the "bluest" color.

The bark is a thick, smooth gray. In old trees it becomes very hard and deeply fissured at the base; the branchlets are shiny.

The needles are definitely four-sided, with a very sharp point. This is the spruce that really pricks your hands if you curl your fingers around a twig.

Cones are abundantly produced, singly or in clusters, drooping from the branch tips. They are 7-10 cm long, golden tan when mature. The scales are thin but tough, wavy along the edge and slightly toothed at the tip.

This is the state tree of Colorado and grows especially well in the mountain chains of the northern Rocky Mountains or in the high areas of the southern Rockies. In Montana and Idaho it is found between elevations of 6,000–9,000 feet, south through the mountains of Colorado to the Sangre de Cristo, Mogollon, and Sacramento Mountains of New Mexico at elevations between 8,000–11,000 feet, in the Uinta and Wasatch Mountains of Utah, and in Arizona in the Kaibab Plateau and White Mountains, between 7,000–11,000 feet elevation.

WEEPING SPRUCE
(Brewer's Spruce)
Picea breweriana

The Weeping Spruce is a rare spruce with a long slender spire-like crown with the higher branches short and up-turned, but many of

the middle branches drooping. The lower branches are mainly horizontal but produce "cord-like" branchlets which hang vertically. There also are many pendulous side branches. These, along with the cord-like branchlets which may be as long as two meters (6'), give the tree a "weeping" appearance.

The bark is thin, quite smooth, reddish-brown with long thin scales. When the scales flake off, they leave a definite scar on the trunk. The trunk base is very thick, the tree tapering quickly.

The needles are rounded, shiny green on the lower surface, but the upper surface is flattened and is whitish with stomata bands on either side of the mid-vein. They are 1.8-2.5 cm long (¾-1''), grow all around the twig, and are not prickly when touched.

The pendulous cones are narrow and oblong, 7-10 cm long (3-4''). The smooth, rounded scales are thin, but the tip is thicker than in other spruces, purplish before maturity, warm brown when ripe. The seeds drop in September and October.

The wood is soft but heavy and close-grained. It is not a common spruce, only found in southwestern Oregon and northwestern California and does not seem to do well in cultivation. Even if it does grow, it grows very slowly. It grows in chilly areas, especially on northern slopes and at canyon heads, from 4,000-7,000 feet elevation. Found in the Coast Ranges, Siskiyous, Trinity, and Klamath Mountains of Oregon and California.

MOUNTAIN HEMLOCK
(Black Hemlock)
Tsuga mertensiana

The tall slender drooping tip or leader of this tree immediately identifies it, giving it a truly unique silhouette. The slender branches also tend to droop, even though their branchlets often arise vertically.

Mountain Hemlock (or Black Hemlock, probably because of the dense foliage) is a tree of the mountains, growing where snow piles deeply. In fact, many Hemlocks on steep slopes are permanently bent near the base because the young trees with slender trunks were easily weighted down with the snow load and they never completely rebounded.

They tend to be small trees, from 8-18 meters (25-60') in height with diameter of 25-50 cm (10-20''), but may grow to be 25 meters tall and 75 cm in diameter. The trunk tapers very rapidly. The tree tends to branch clear to the ground, old trees often having a "ruffle" of branches around their base even if the trunk is bare up a ways, or they have at least one or two low branches. The bark of young trees becomes rough and furrowed very early, while in old trees, though the bark may appear blue-gray from a distance, its furrows change to dark red-brown or even purplish.

From a distance the foliage appears deep blue-green or green and "soft" because of the even size of the needles and their arrangement. Though they are growing from all sides of the twig, they seem to be brushed slightly upwards and towards the branch tips. They have stomate bands on both surfaces. The blunt needles are short and each is on a short stem which remains on the branch when the needle falls in its fourth year.

Mountain Hemlocks produce abundant cones each year, often hanging in thick clusters on most of the branches. The cones are usually smallish and very light weight with thin, rounded scales. They vary, however, and may be as small as 1 cm or as long as 7 cm, but are usually 2-5 cm (1-2'').

This timberline tree, which in the Arctic is at sea level, extends from the mountains of Alaska south in the alpine zone through Washington and Oregon and the Sierra Nevada of California and east into northern Idaho and Montana where it is high, cold, and moist and prefers the northern slopes

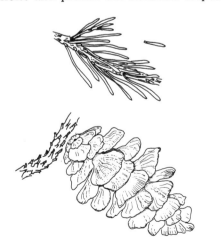

WESTERN HEMLOCK
Tsuga heterophylla

The Western Hemlock is a beautiful forest tree which should be planted more in parks and spacious gardens for it is a lovely tree in shape and leaf spray. It may grow to be 60 meters tall (180'), though more usually from 30-50 meters (90-150'). It has a narrow crown with a slender flexible tip, and upper branch ends are also exceedingly flexible and tend to droop. This drooping tip and upper branches are characteristic of its silhouette. Old trees will still retain the flexible branch tips, though the branches tend to sweep downwards as they age and the top may become broken.

The trunk may grow to be 2-3 meters in diameter (6-9'). The mature bark is 2.5-4 cm thick, with deep fissures dividing the wide flat ridges which have thin copper-brown scales. Bark on young trees and branches is smooth gray with a hint of red.

The branchlets are pale yellow at first, then darkish red, fuzzy with hairs (hold spray tip to light or use a hand magnifier). The branches and branchlets are flat and are closely spaced

The needles are jointed on a very short stalk (not persistent pegs as on spruces) and usually twist at the base enough so the spray is flat-appearing. They are closely spaced and are dark green on the upper surface, but the lower surface appears silvery because of the two broad whitish bands of stomata. There is a definite groove down the middle of the upper surface. The needles are round-tipped and vary in length on the same twig from .6-2 cm in length

(¼-¾ "), the shorter ones growing from the upper part of the twig, the longer ones growing from the lower surface.

The wood is pale yellow-brown, light but hard and tough. It is a good wood for building, for it hardens and darkens with age. The bark is also useful for a tanning agent; its fibers useful for paper pulp and rayon.

This is the most common tree in the damp rainy areas of the northwest. It grows along the coast from southern Alaska (where it is particularly abundant) to northern California's fog belt mountains. East through southern British Columbia and Washington to the Bitterroots of Idaho and on the western slopes of the Oregon Cascades. It needs plenty of rain, and lives from sea level to 5,000 feet.

DOUGLAS FIR
(Oregon Pine)
Pseudotsuga menziesii (taxifolia)

Douglas Fir is one of the biggest and most common forest trees of the Pacific Northwest, often growing 60-70 meters tall and 1-3 meters in diameter. Further south or higher in the mountains they may be smaller. Douglas Fir is not a fir, though the needles remind one of the White Fir; nor is it a hemlock (as part of its scientific name suggests) though early botanists put it in that group. It is not a pine for its needles are arranged singly on the branch and the bases are not wrapped. Actually it was finally named as a separate genus, *Pseudotsuga* (meaning false hemlock).

The cone is the unique feature of this genus, and is the thing to look for. It is cinnamon brown, and has scales as do most cone-bearing trees, but extending between and beyond them are peculiar 3-pronged or toothed narrow bracts. The cone is fairly light weight, 6-9 cm long and 2-3 cm broad with thinnish scales.

As a young tree it has a smooth gray bark with tiny blisters, but as it grows it develops an exceedingly thick, corky bark, deeply fissured, with broad ridges. It is very fibrous and can withstand fire. Its abundant light seed makes it one of the first conifers to grow in a burned-over area.

The trees are fast-growing and soon produce a very symmetrical, pyramidal tree. There are many long side branches with the lower ones drooping, the upper ones straight out or turning upwards. An old tree may develop a broad crown.

The needles are flat, slightly grooved on the upper surface, and usually bluntish. Though arranged around the twig, the needle base

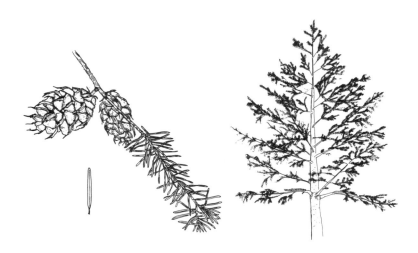

twists to make a more or less flat spray. The foliage is usually deep yellow-green but may be even blue-green.

Douglas Fir may grow in nearly pure stands or in mixed evergreen forests, preferring the more or less sheltered, cooler slopes and canyons. It adapts to many soil conditions and succeeds well with different species in different habitats. In southern Oregon and California, it grows mainly with Yellow Pine, Sugar Pine, White Fir and Incense Cedar except in the Coast Ranges where it is abundant among Redwood, Tanbark Oak, and Madrone. In northern Oregon and Washington it grows mainly with Western Hemlock, Western Red Cedar, Yellow Pine, and with Western White Pine, Larch and Lodgepole Pine nearer the coast. It is widely distributed over western North America from British Columbia south to Mexico. It is most abundant and biggest in Washington and Oregon, but common in Sierran and coastal California, south and east to Arizona, southern New Mexico and northwestern Texas. It extends east from Canada into Idaho, Montana, Utah, South Dakota, and Colorado.

BIG CONE DOUGLAS FIR
(Big Cone Spruce)
Pseudotsuga macrocarpa

Although a common name for this is Big Cone Spruce it is not a spruce, nor does it look particularly like one since its needles are not on persistent "pegs" which is *the* characteristic of spruces, and

its needles are definitely arranged in a 2-ranked way with a flat spray. The name Big Cone Douglas Fir is very suitable for both its cones and foliage resemble Douglas Fir *(Pseudotsuga menziesii)*. The cones, however are much bigger (10-22 cm; 4-8''), and though it has the typical 3-prong bract, it does not extend as far beyond the scales. This tree does not become the enormous forest tree that *P. menziesii* does.

The branches are long and at right angles from the trunk, extending outwards, usually horizontally, with only the lower ones drooping at the ends.

The bark on mature trees is thick (15 cm), is a dark red-brown or almost charcoal. The ridges are broad and scaly between the furrows. The branchlets are powdery when seen through a hand magnifier, but this disappears and the twigs become smooth and gray.

The needles are deep blue-green, arranged in a very flat spray by a twist at the needle base. They are usually 2-3 cm long, but often are very irregular in length on the same twig—from 1-4 cm. There is a noticeable line down their upper surface.

The green bracts on young cones are tinged with red; the cone, when mature, is dark brown. The typical 3-prong bract just barely sticks out beyond the broad thin scales. The cone may be 10-22 cm long, (4-8½''). The wood is hard and close-grained.

Big Cone Douglas Fir grows only in southern California on the cooler slopes and canyons south from the Santa Inez mountains to the Cuyamacas in San Diego County between 2,200 and 7,000 feet elevation. It extends into Baja California. It is found with chaparral, Yellow Pine and Coulter Pine. It is not found in the Sierra Nevada of California.

FIRS

Key To Species of Firs

1 a. Needles dark green above; white stomate bands only on *lower* surface . . .   go to #2

   b. Needles blue-green; stomata on both sides . . .   go to #4

2 a. Needles bristle-tipped, flat, rigid, 3-5.5 cm long; cones with long narrow bracts extending beyond scales—Santa Lucia Fir, *Abies bracteata* . . .   turn to page 68

   b. Needles not bristle-tipped . . .   go to #3

3 a. Needles 2-ranked, *flat* green sprays—Lowland or Grand Fir, *Abies grandis* . . .   turn to page 67

   b. Needles curving over twigs showing very silvery undersurface, very *fat* spray—Pacific Silver or Lovely Fir, *Abies amabilis* . . .   turn to page 71

4 a. Needles flat . . .   go to #5

   b. Needles 4-sided . . .   go to #6

5 a. Needles on lower branches twist at base to form a flattish spray; needles 2-6 cm long; upper bark whitish, lower bark rough and fissured—White Fir, *Abies concolor* . . .   turn to page 65

   b. Needles 1.5-2.5 cm long; bark hard, flinty, thin, ashy-gray, very narrow silhouette—Alpine or Sub-alpine Fir, *Abies lasiocarpa* . . .   turn to page 70

6 a. Needles with groove only on upper surface; thinnish bark; cone with long bracts folding down over scales—Noble Fir, *Abies procera (nobilis)* . . .   turn to page 72

   b. Needles with distinct groove on both top and bottom; thick, red, platy, scaly, fissured bark. Bract on cones not noticeable—Red Fir, *Abies magnifica* . . .   turn to page 66

WHITE FIR
(Balsam)
Abies concolor

White Fir is a stiff, symmetrical pale blue-green tree with the needles on the lower branches twisting at the base so they seem to form a flat spray. It grows as tall as 70 meters (210') with the trunk up to 1.5-2 meters (4.5-6') in diameter. Branches tend to be stout, short, and the lower ones droop, but the rest are horizontal and regularly branching from the trunk in whorls. The top of the tree is very narrow.

Young trees and upper branches have smooth silvery-white bark with resin blisters marking the surface. Mature trees have deep fissures in the very thick, ashy, gray-brown bark.

The gray-green needles vary in length from 2-6 cm (.7-2.3''), with the ones on lower branches the longest. The upper needles have a definite rib or ridge on their inner surface, and tend to curve up around the branch, but they are not as thickly grouped as on Red Fir. From a distance the foliage on the whole tree tends to give a whitish-or grayish-green appearance.

The cones are upright, rounded at the top, 7-12 cm high (2.5.5''), 2.5-4 cm wide (1-1.75''), greenish or purplish, and becomes brown when mature. They are often so full of pine resin that they sparkle in the sun. The scales separate and fall, releasing the seeds in the early autumn.

The White fir grows on mountain slopes and rocky areas from 3,000 feet to 7,000 feet elevation usually, though up to 10,000 feet in the southern part of its range. It seems to thrive in drier areas

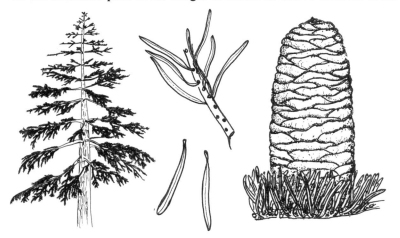

and at lower elevations than the Red Fir. It mostly grows with Yellow Pine, and is found from northern Oregon east to the Rocky Mountains of Idaho, Utah, and Colorado, south to Arizona, New Mexico, and Mexico. It is also found in the higher mountains of Nevada, northern and southern California ranges and Baja California, and abundantly in the Sierra Nevada.

RED FIR
(Silver Tip)
Abies magnifica

Red Firs often grow into large, magnificent trees (the species name suggests this), usually 20-60 meters tall (60-180'), though they may reach to 70 meters and 1-2 meters in diameter (3-6'). It is a very regular-branching tree with whorls of four or five branches at one place, with a very even distance between side branches. There is almost a snowflake pattern developed by its branchlets. Old trees even retain these features.

The branches tend to be short and thick, drooping except near the top where they are stiffly symmetrical. Young trees have a very light chalky-gray bark with resin pockets that look like blisters. This is true of the branches and upper trunk of mature trees also, abruptly grading from this to the thick, dark, red-brown, deeply fissured bark on the lower trunk of mature trees. The ridges are wider than the fissures and tend to be rounded and the whole thing diagonally furrowed in a very characteristic way.

The needles are short (1.5 cm) and are four-sided. An especially noticeable ridge runs down the center of the inner surface, the outer surface being more rounded with the ridges near the edges. The needles are bent from the lower side so they tend to make each branch appear as though all grew from the top side, producing a fat, rounded spray. Needles on the lower branches are somewhat flatter, longer and more blunt at the tip, making a more open spray than the tightly bent and shorter, crowded needles on the upper branches. The foliage is dense, blue-green, with the new growth especially having a whitish tinge.

The small male flowers are purplish, hanging from the under side of the upper branches. The purplish female cones stand erect on the upper branches, maturing in one season. They are 13-20 cm tall (5-8'') and 6-9 cm thick (2.5-3.5''). They are ripe by late summer (August) and in September the scales begin falling. The seed with its shiny wing is triangular in shape, 2.5 cm in length.

Young trees are often raised and/or cut for Silver Tip Christmas

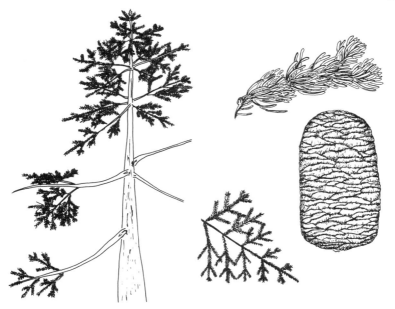

trees because of their frosted or whitish tinge and their symmetrical form.

Grows on ridges and slopes, including windswept ones, from southern Oregon in the Cascades and Siskiyous and the northern Coast Ranges of California south in the Sierra Nevada, particularly on the west side, often in almost pure stands, but also among Lodgepoles and Black Hemlock between 5,000 and 9,000 feet elevation. It will grow up to timberline, but is most magnificent around meadows and on gentle slopes.

GRAND FIR
(Giant Fir, Lowland Fir)
Abies grandis

The name Grand Fir comes from the fact that this fir can be very tall and imposing with beautiful long branches which first droop, then lift near the end. The many short side branchlets produce an opened-fan appearance at the branch end. It is sometimes called White Fir, a name which really belongs to *Abies concolor*, because of its light-colored bark. The Grand Fir can be distinguished from the true White Fir by its dark green leaves on the upper surface and the whitish stomate bands on the lower surface.

As a forest tree it may grow to 90 meters (270'), but it more commonly grows to between 30 and 60 meters (90-180') with a diameter

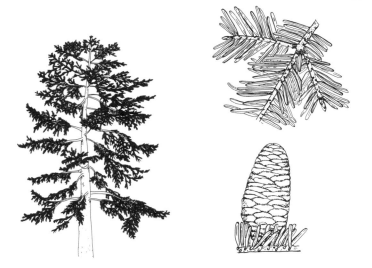

of less than a meter. The trunk grows very straight and only gradually tapers. Only as a large tree does the smooth ashy-gray trunk become regularly but shallowly fissured, the flat areas still showing gray areas. As the tree matures, the bark becomes very hard reddish brown, still retains a grayish cast, and becomes more deeply fissured.

Needles are 2.5-5.5 cm long, the petioles twisting so they form a 2-ranked flat spray. As with many other firs, those needles on the upper surface are shorter than those attached further under the twig. The needles have a tiny notch in the tip where the mid-vein ends. This isn't always noticeable, however, unless you flatten the needle, for the very tip tends to bend down. The upper surface is deep shiny green with two lightish bands of stomata on the lower surface, but these are not as wide or white as in *Abies bracteata*. The needles on the upper part of the tree are much shorter and tend to be all the same length (2.5 cm), crowded together.

Grows in mixed evergreen forests and coastal forests from British Columbia east to Montana and south through Washington and Oregon to the Coast Ranges of northern California.

SANTA LUCIA FIR
(Bristlecone Fir)
Abies bracteata (venusta)

The Santa Lucia Fir is a rare tree in that it only grows naturally in the Santa Lucia Mountains near Monterey, California. It has a

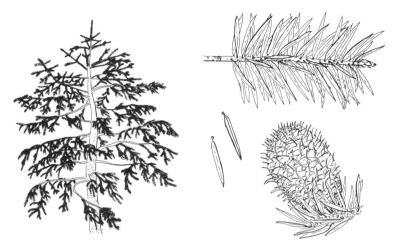

long narrow crown, the tree growing 30-50 meters tall (90-150'). The branches seem to be less stiff than many firs and tend to grow downwards or droop rather than standing out stiffly. Often the branching starts just above the ground level. This, plus the long narrow crown and the very sharp top, gives it a distinctive silhouette. The needles are long, and with the underside so white, the tree develops a characteristic "silvery" appearance.

The young twigs are somewhat whitish, turning smooth, clear brown. The bark is light brown with tight scales.

The flat, stiff needles are dark green on the upper surface, silvery with wide bands of stomates on the under surface, with a green mid-rib and green edge. The needles gradually taper to a sharp point and are 3-5.5 cm long (1.25-2.25"). The needles, when young, are very light green on the upper surface and very white on the lower surface. The attachment of the needle to the twig is particularly large. Petioles of the needles are twisted so the needles are 2-ranked or produce a flat spray. All of the needles are exceptionally long and wide for a fir.

The mature purple-brown cones are very unusual in that the middle lobe of the tan bract that underlies the scale is long and narrow and extends past the scale.

Grows on rocky slopes and canyons from 2,000 to 4,500 feet, with mixed conifers. Found only in the Santa Lucia Mountains of Monterey County, California, but because it is an exceptionally beautiful tree, it is often and widely planted as specimen trees.

It is interesting that three conifers, the Monterey Pine *(Pinus radiata)*, the Monterey Cypress *(Cupressus macrocarpa)*, and the

Santa Lucia Fir *(Abies bracteata)* are each only found in the very small area in, around, or somewhat north and south of Monterey.

ALPINE FIR
(Sub-alpine Fir, Balsam Fir)
Abies lasiocarpa

Alpine Fir is a small, high altitude fir, not seen as often as most other firs. It has an exceptionally long, narrow, conical trunk—more so than any of the other trees with which it grows, so is easily recognized from a distance. It often grows to be 20-30 meters (60-90') tall, but in the higher exposed places, it may be under two meters (6') tall. Usually in those situations, the lower branches are very long and lie on the ground.

The bark is only slightly rough or fissured near the base. Most of it is thin, hard, flinty, and quite smooth, ashy gray to chalky white.

The branches are very dense and droop, often to the ground. The needles are shiny bluish-green, the young ones quite silvery, 1.5-2.5 cm long (.5-1''). They are flat and blunt, except those near the top of the tree which are somewhat pointed and shorter. The upper surface of the twig is crowded with upwards-pointing needles, those on sides and bottom twist to point upwards also.

The purple cones are fairly slender and small, 3-4 cm (1.25-1.5'') wide and 5-10 cm (2-4'') tall. They gradually get lighter-colored till they mature and the fan-shaped scales start falling.

The wood is usually not too useful because of the branching-to-the-ground characteristic. The Alpine Fir grows in valleys, on slopes, and on ridges from southeastern Alaska through British

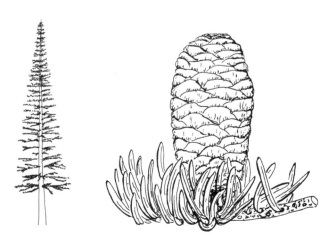

Columbia and western Alberta south through Washington, Oregon, Idaho, and western Montana and Wyoming to southern Arizona and New Mexico.

PACIFIC SILVER FIR
Abies amabilis

The Pacific Silver Fir is found most often on well-drained slopes of canyons, from southeastern Alaska (where it grows from sea level to 1,000 feet elevation) down through the coastal mountains and the Cascades of British Columbia, Washington, and Oregon up to progressively higher elevations (from 2,000 to 7,000 feet) around the Crater Lake area. It is often planted as a specimen tree.

Its common name comes from its habitat along the Pacific Ocean, and from the very silvery-appearing underside of the needles and the whitish, smooth bark. The needle buds are characteristically very resin-covered.

The bark, except for the base of mature trees, is smooth, ashy-gray with almost chalky-white patches. The base of old trunks is reddish-brown, scaly and seamy. In forests, these straight trees, clear of branches for a ⅓ of the height, may be 60 meters tall (180'), with a very slender, spire-like tip (so they may look similar to the Alpine Fir *(A. lasiocarpa)*. The branches all droop, curving down, then outwards.

The needles of the lower part of the tree are not at all crowded together, but are spaced along the branchlets. Needles on the lower twig surface twist to be almost horizontal, while those on the upper surface bend forward, giving a 2-way-combed appearance that is very typical. They are 3 cm (1.25") long, flat and either blunt or slightly notched at the tip, with a groove along the dark green shiny upper surface. The underside is silvery white with stomates, except for the mid-rib and the rolled margins.

Needles on the upper branches of the tree, particularly those with cones, are very different. They are thickish, shorter (2 cm), pointed at the tip, stand upwards and are densely crowded.

The beautiful cones are 10-15 cm long (4-6"), 6 cm in diameter (2.5") and dark velvety purple with smooth, rounded scales.

NOBLE FIR
Abies procera (nobilis)

The Noble Fir is a tall, very symmetrical, stiff-looking, very dense tree of the Coast Ranges and Cascades of Washington and Oregon, and the Siskiyous of northern California, growing best where there is plenty of moisture. Usually grows with Douglas Fir, Western Hemlock, and Western White Pine. The trunks tend to be very straight, with no branches for quite a ways. Its usual height is 45-65 meters (140-200'), with a diameter of .75-2 meters (30-72'').

The branches are short, stiff, and crowded, and stand out horizontally, making a very "dense" tree. The stiff needles are closely spaced, grooved, and all twist as though they were brushed upwards. The needles on lower branches are longer (about 2.5 cm), flattened and with a small notch at the tip. Those on upper branches are short, very angled on the back, and sharp-pointed. Both kinds are very densely arranged, all curve to stand erect on the twig, and all are a silvery, bluish-green from the stomate bands.

This fir produces a very large, unusual cone—it may be up to 17 cm long (6.5''). The wide, protruding bracts have long slender mid-ribs. Each bract with its long point bends abruptly and hangs down, seeming to "shingle" the scales. The cones are yellow-green to yellow-brown when they ripen in September.

SEQUOIA
(Sierra Redwood, Big-tree)
Sequoiadendron gigantea

The Sequoia is a well-known tree because of its beauty, size, age, and the need to protect the remaining few "giants." It is of very limited distribution now—there are only about 75 scattered groves on the western slope of the Sierra Nevada in California from the southern part of Placer County to Kern County—roughly in the south central part of the western Sierra. There may be as much as forty or fifty miles between groves in the northern part of its range.

The best-known groves are the Mariposa Big Trees (part of Yosemite National Park) and in Sequoia National Park.

The bark, especially at the base of huge old trees, is very thick, deeply furrowed and with wide ridges—somewhat similar to the Coast Redwood except this bark is deeper, wider, and thicker, and is a marvelous cinnamon-red color. It is also fibrous and spongy-soft, and bits are continually breaking off. Masses of litter accumulate under the trees. Young trees and branches have thin, scaly bark, which is grayish or purplish in color.

The leaves are scale-like with their lower ends closely attached and lying along the twig, the upper end sharp and sticking slightly out except on the twig tips, or on the larger stems where they will be small and close-fitting. They are definitely blue-green in color, making a nice contrast to the red bark.

The cones resemble enlarged Coast Redwood cones, usually about 5-8 cm long (2-3''), 3 cm wide, reddish-brown. The cone scales are "squashed-diamond" shape and only separate slightly from each other to let the seeds escape, not turning outwards as do pines. The cones do not fall when ripe; they are often cut down by the hundreds at that time by the squirrels, but normally they would stay on the tree for 8-10 years, and their stems even show growth rings. The seeds are very tiny and light—91,000 to make a pound.

It prefers to grow on low ridges and slopes near the heads of streams, practically never in exposed areas. With enough moisture, it seems to grow well in many different types of soils. It may grow with Sugar Pines, Douglas Fir, White Fir, but may also be in almost pure groves. In its northern pockets, it is at 5,000 feet elevation, gradually increasing to 8,500 feet as you go southward.

REDWOOD
Sequoia sempervirens

Redwood is a large, beautiful coastal tree, grown as a specimen tree in many parts of the world, (where it can survive) because of its beautiful growth, leaves, trunk, etc. Usually they are from 60-90 meters tall (180-270'), but may be taller and so large that many people have to hold hands to reach around its huge base.

Young trees grow very rapidly, developing a narrow conical silhouette—the upper branches trending up, lower ones drooping. As it grows older, it looses this shape, and often there will be several large, somewhat drooping, horizontal branches with several small ones. One interesting characteristic is its ability to produce root shoots—often you can find slender shoots coming up around the main trunk. If the tree is cut or burned out, these shoots may develop into big trees. Many areas are now seen with rings of redwoods—the original tree is gone from the middle, and the shoots are now the big trees.

The cones are small (1.5-2 cm), and the scales open more widely to let the seeds out than the Giant Sequoia does, but otherwise it re-

sembles a miniature one of those cones. The cones are produced on short side branches with much shorter needles, the leaves immediately below the cone being scale-like. The lower leaves on the side twigs are also small and scale-like. The regular leaves are evergreen flat needles, varying in size from 1 to almost 3 cm long, stiff and fairly sharp-pointed, and usually more or less opposite each other to form a somewhat flat spray. The leaf bases are closely attached to the twig and extend down the twig a ways. The main twig tips—the growing ends—have very reduced needles, some of which are really long-pointed scales resembling those of *Sequoiadendron gigantea*.

Redwoods grow from southwestern Oregon south to Monterey, and are especially abundant in the northern Coast Ranges of California. Naturally it is never more than about twenty miles from the ocean, preferring fog belts, and ranging from sea level to about 2,500 feet in elevation.

INCENSE CEDAR
Calocedrus (Libocedrus) decurrens

Incense Cedar is a distinctive beautiful forest tree with a broad base, rapidly tapering to the tip at 25-40 meters (100-160'). The

trunk is rough, the bark a beautiful warm cinnamon-brown, fibrous and grooved 5-7 cm thick (2-3'') on the lower portion. Young trees have thin, smoothish, cinnamon-red bark, somewhat scaly. The upper branches point upwards, the lower branches curve down, with the flat branchlets hanging vertically.

The light yellow-green needles are small and scale-like, overlapping in pairs. The side pair is much larger and almost hides the inner tiny pair. Only the tips are free, with the rest extending down the stem a ways. The scales are usually about .3 cm long, but on actively-growing tips, they may be as long as 1 cm. Older twigs are not quite as flat, but the same distinctive larger side pair of scales almost covering the inner pair makes a recognizable pattern—producing a flat twig. Though the twig is small, it alternates between wide and narrow, depending on the position of the free tip and closely-attached lower part of each scale.

Numerous small male flowers are produced at twig tips; the female flowers are on different twigs of the same branch and develop into small woody cones made of 3 paired scales. One set is small at the base, another pair is much larger with the two scales facing each other and opening widely, exposing the central upright partition made of the third pair of scales. The two seeds are held between the second and third pairs of scales, falling when this unique cone opens. The seeds are small, with wings almost as large as the cone scale. The cones hang from the pendulous twigs, maturing the first autumn, and are deep red-brown in color when open.

The wood is fine-grained and fairly pale, though it may be reddish, and is very durable even when perforated by disease (mostly fungi). It has a pleasant though fairly strong odor.

Incense Cedar is abundant in the Cascades of Oregon, the Sierra Nevada and inner Coast Ranges of California to Baja California and the western edge of Nevada. It grows from 2,500 feet to 6,000 feet elevation, especially with Yellow Pine.

WESTERN RED CEDAR
(Canoe Cedar)
Thuja plicata

The Western Red Cedar belongs to the group of evergreens with tiny scale-like leaves knows as "arbor vitae." They are commonly called cedars, but they are not true cedars.

The dark yellow-green shiny scales are minutely overlapping, arranged as is *Calocedrus*—the first pair with a longish point and the next pair smaller and at right angles to the first pair. The scales,

twigs and sprays are *flat*, the whole branch hanging vertically and gracefully as a drape. The side twigs on each twig will be further branched, but these will almost exclusively be on one side—the side towards the tip—so a very regular, patterned arrangement results.

The tree may become very large, up to 65 meters (195'), and 1-2 meters in diameter (3-6'), often buttressed at the base. There are many branches, mostly at right angles to the trunk, then swooping down, the branchlet tips turning up. The branches are smooth, but have some long fissures. The main trunk is dull red-brown with long, vertically twisting, fissures which are stringy and fibrous.

The small woody cones are usually made of eight or nine scales, each pair alternating at right angles with the preceding one, resembling a compounded Incense Cedar cone. The cones bend sharply away and up from the slender twig that produces them. The cone is about 1 cm long, and many are produced on the upper (outer) surface near the tip of the flat sprays. Last year's open cones may still be on the twig, back from the tip.

Western Red Cedar is also called Canoe Cedar because that's one use the Indians of the Northwest had for this giant tree—giant canoes as much as 22 meters (67') were made from them. They also carved their totem poles from the huge trunks.

Grows from Alaska south, both along the coast and inland to 6,000 feet elevation, in the Washington Olympics and west slope of the Cascades to 4,000 feet, the Canadian Rockies, Alberta and eastern British Columbia south to the Bitterroots of Idaho and Montana from 2,000–7,000 feet, and in Oregon's Coast Ranges and Cascades to 7,500 feet and into the fog belt of northern California.

CYPRESS
Cupressus

Cypress trees in the west are an interesting group with many species, but each grows in a fairly restricted area of southern Oregon, California or Arizona. They are, however, widely planted elsewhere. A few have been included here that are somewhat known and/or have greater range than the others.

They are aromatic trees with thick, stringy, fibrous bark, round twigs with small scale-like overlapping leaves, and are closely related to the *Chamaecyparis* genus. Cypresses have quadrangular or round branches, not flat branches, and the branching is irregular, not in one plane.

The oblong or roundish cones, usually 1.5-3 cm long, are woody, with close-fitting (not over-lapping) scales which mature the second year, but sometimes not opening for years. Each scale produces 15-20 seeds with hard narrow wings.

MONTEREY CYPRESS
Cupressus macrocarpa

Although the Monterey Cypress only grows naturally in a very limited area around Carmel, south of Monterey Bay in California, it is well-known because of its picturesque growth on windswept sea cliffs, and because it is planted in many localities. It grows 15-25 meters tall (45-75') with a trunk which may become twisted and contorted, often up to 2 meters in diameter. The thick fibrous bark is very characteristic of mature trees.

The scale-like yellow-green leaves are tiny (3 mm) on the round twigs, larger back from the actively-growing tip. The male flowers are tiny and yellow, at twig-tips, opening in March and April. The female flower is not noticeable at first, but develops in two years

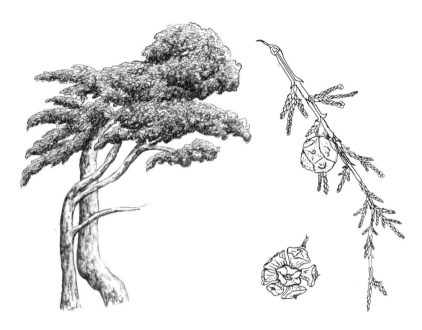

into a slightly oblong woody cone 2.5-3.5 cm long, usually one to a branchlet, but sometimes two or three in a bunch. The squarish cone scales do not overlap, but fit tightly together in the immature cone, each scale having a definite curved hump in its center. The scales finally open widely to release the seeds, the cone remaining on the tree for a long time afterwards.

ARIZONA CYPRESS
(Roughbark Cypress)
Cupressus arizonica

This is a beautiful cypress of southern Arizona, characterized by shreddy bark as it grows old, exposing the dark red inner bark. Young branches and stems are smooth and red but the bark at the base of the mature trunk is thick and dark gray, dark brown or even blackish. It is deeply fissured into long ridges, and is fibrous or shreddy.

A very similar tree *C. glabra* grows in central Arizona, except that as it ages it keeps its smooth red bark, just peeling off layers, never developing the thick, fissured, dark trunk.

Arizona Cypress may grow to be 10-20 meters (30-60') tall, often as a very dense tree with a straight thick trunk. The tiny scale-like

leaves are sharply pointed on the back, usually gray-green except for the blue-green young foliage.

At first the cones are green, then dull brown to purplish; when mature they weather to a soft gray. They are about 2.5 cm (1'') in diameter, with 6-8 scales, each with a definite umbo. Each cone produces many seeds—about 100.

This tree is often used as a Christmas tree in the southwest, especially because its scale-like leaves do not fall off as quickly as conifers with needle-like leaves. It is an excellent tree in semi-dry areas that get at least 15'' of rain and not too extended periods of cold.

Arizona Cypress grows well in southeastern Arizona, on the mountains from 3,500–7,000 feet.

SARGENT CYPRESS
Cupressus sargentii

Sargent's Cypress, though found only in California, is more widespread than many cypresses, for it is found from Santa Barbara in the south to Mendocino County in the north. It is found in ravines and on rocky ridges in chaparral areas or with the "closed cone" pines, often on the higher peaks such as Mt. Tamalpais.

There is usually just one straight main trunk, the branches erect or spreading, but tending to form a conical tree when young. As it grows older it becomes more open and spreading and usually flat-topped. The bark is thick and fibrous, usually a very dark brown. The twigs tend to be very short, with regular but very stiff branching. The minute dark green, scale-like leaves are blunt, often dusty-looking and very closely attached on the cord-like twig. The woody, roundish cone of 6-10 scales is small, often just 2.0-2.5 cm (¾-1''), and glossy brown when ripe in its second autumn, wea-

CHAMAECYPARIS
False-Cypress

The name *Chamaecyparis* literally means "little cypress." Sometimes, species of *Chamaecyparis* are called cedars, but more often they are called cypresses as a common name.

The *Chamaecyparis* is a group of very important forest trees and are very closely related to the cypresses. This group produces round twigs, as do true cypresses, but these grow in a definite flat spray. The branching also is flat—in one plane. The fast-growing tips of some are flattish, but back from the tip, the twigs are round.

The small scale-like leaves are arranged like the *Thujas* which also have flat branches, but here the scale leaves are narrower, finer, and the scales are not toothed.

The female flowers develop into small (1 cm), spherical, erect, woody cones with only a few scales, opening widely in the summer to drop two to five seeds per scale. The cones continue to stay on the tree for long periods of time. It is not uncommon to see old, opened cones, fair-sized maturing cones, and the newly developing female flowers all on one spray at once. The cones easily distinguish them from the *Thujas* and the larger woody cones of cypresses.

They may grow on exposed mountain tops or slopes, and never get to be big forest trees. They are especially abundant in the northwest.

LAWSON CYPRESS
(Port Orford Cedar)
Chamaecyparis lawsoniana

Lawson Cypress as a young tree is dense in an almost perfect conical shape—no long whip-like leader as in *Chamaecyparis nootkatensis* nor like the slender tip of Western Red Cedar *Thuja plicata*. When older, it may grow to 60 meters (180') with much of that clear of branches.

The foliage is bright yellowish-green, and all the tips and branchlets are flat (not just the tips, as in Alaskan Cypress). The tiny scale leaves overlap in pairs. The scales have a small gland which is seen as a tiny dot on the flat upper surface.

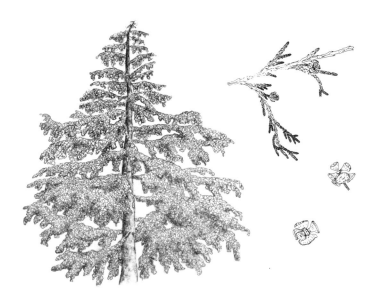

The bark is thick and reddish-brown with long vertical fissures between narrow but rounded stringy ridges. There are less distinct cross fissures, but the surface is broken into long plates and is somewhat scaly. The young branches are quite smooth. Because of this bark and its flat sprays, it may be mistaken for Western Red Cedar, but the cones are very different, and the undersurface of Western Red Cedar is dull green while Lawson Cypress is often whitish beneath.

The tiny round woody cones are bluish-purple when young (almost like tiny juniper berries), then become green, changing to cinnamon-brown when ripe and opening widely so the 6 scales are then easily seen.

Lawson Cypress is also called Port Orford Cedar. It is mainly a coastal tree, found from southern Oregon to the Klamath River north of San Francisco, but inland in the Siskiyous of Oregon and on the headwaters of the Sacramento River in California.

ALASKAN CYPRESS
(Yellow Cypress)
Chamaecyparis nootkatensis

The Alaskan Cypress is a beautiful tree with its gray-green or blue-green branches arranged in pendulous flat sprays, and many tiny round woody cones which hang on after the seeds are shed. It

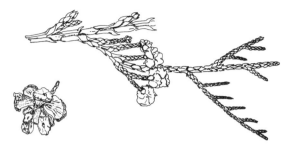

has thin (1-2 cm) brownish-gray bark irregularly fissured and broken into flat ridges with large loose scales. The bark of mature trees may be folded or fluted near the base; the upper bark is grayer and shows diagonal fissures and flakes in narrow strips. It might be mistaken for Western Red Cedar because of the flat sprays, but the bark is different, the scale-like leaves are smaller.

Alaskan Cypress develops a conical shape, except the tree tip is whip-like and usually bends over. The whole tree, with its drooping branches, gives it a "weeping" silhouette. Grows from 25-30 meters tall (75-90') and from 1-1.5 meters thick (3-4').

The tiny scale-like leaves are arranged in two similar overlapping pairs; the scales on the branchlet stems are much larger. The tip growth is quite flat, but the twigs are round and look much like true cypresses. The *Chamaecyparis* group is called false-cypress and for good reason—they *are* very similar; however in this group the sprays are flat and the cones bear only a few seeds for each scale and are mature in just one year. Alaskan Cypress resembles Lawson Cypress but the Lawson Cypress has branchlets and twigs that are round, and each scale-leaf bears a definite gland. Also the Lawson Cypress has a thick pyramidal top and is definitely yellow-green or at least not blue-green.

The male flowers are tiny and are on side branchlets; the female flowers are very tiny and are further out on the branchlet sprays. They develop into round, 6-scaled cones which mature the first year, opening in late summer or fall to drop their seeds. These cones, about 1 cm across, stay on the tree so you can see brown open cones on last year's growth and new green ones on this year's.

It is generally found along streams, in valleys, and on mountain slopes, but also grows in exposed areas and is usually very stunted there. It is usually found with Sitka Spruce, Western Red Cedar, Western Hemlock in Washington, British Columbia and southern Alaska up to 3,000 feet.

JUNIPER
Juniperus

Key To Species of Junipers

1 a. Leaves tiny, scale-like . . .   go to #2

   b. Leaves awl- or lance-like, in 3's, standing
       out from twig—Dwarf Juniper, *Juniperus
       communis* . . .   turn to page 91

2 a. Berries large, red-brown with sweet pulp . . . go to #3

   b. Berries small, blue or blue-black (with
       bloom), resinous pulp . . .   go to #5

3 a. Bark very checkered and regular like
       alligator. Very large berries—Alligator
       Juniper, *Juniperus deppeana* . . .   turn to page 90

   b. Bark stringy and grayish . . .   go to #4

4 a. Juniper of mid-elevations, western Sierra
       and south; yellow-green, pitted scale leaves
       in 3's—California Juniper, *Juniperus cali-
       fornica* . . .   turn to page 87

   b. Juniper eastward from Sierras; yellow-green
       scale leaves; no pits—Utah Juniper, *Juni-
       perus oesteosperma* . . .   turn to page 85

5 a. 1-seeded, bluish, very small berries (less than
       .5 cm) (may be coppery under bloom)—One-
       seeded Juniper, *Juniperus monosperma* . . . turn to page 89

   b. Twigs and branches droop; gray-blue
       foliage; bright bluish berry; brown bark—
       Rocky Mountain Juniper, *Juniperus scopu-
       lorum* . . .   turn to page 88

   c. Pitted gray-green foliage in 3's; rusty
       cinnamon bark; blue-black berry—Western
       Juniper, *Juniperus occidentalis* . . .   turn to page 85

UTAH JUNIPER
Juniperus (utahensis) oesteosperma

The species name has recently been changed, but the common name still remains Utah Juniper. It has tiny scale-like leaves on the round, compact twigs. They do not have glands or pits.

The tree usually forms a rounded, compact clump 2-4 meters tall, often with many short trunks and side branches, but it may be 1-sided with the thin, whitish, ridged trunk twisting grotesquely. The wood is light yellowish-brown with white sapwood.

Utah Juniper is found in southwestern Wyoming, Nevada, Utah, western Colorado to southeastern California and northwestern Arizona in the higher elevations (5,000–8,000 feet), desert foothills, and mountain slopes where it is rocky or sandy.

WESTERN JUNIPER
(Sierran Juniper, Yellow or Western Red Cedar)
Juniperus occidentalis

Here is an example of a juniper having *cedar* as one of its common names. This is mostly a high mountain, often gnarled tree.

Though it is very like the California Juniper in leaf and bark, that tree is regularly found at a much lower elevation.

The tiny gray-green scale-like leaves fit very tightly on the round twig, arranged in 3's (sometimes in pairs). The pitted white gland on the upper scale surface is very noticeable. The young scale leaves at actively-growing twig ends tend to be much longer and sharper than those lower down. The scale leaves on the old twigs are quite large, distinctly showing the 3-arrangement by the 6 row pattern that develops. Leaves usually die after the second season and are gradually pushed off the branchlet. These older branchlets then tend to show a smooth, thin, reddish bark. The bark of the main trunk and big branches is firm but stringy, light cinnamon-brown in color 1-3 cm thick. It develops widely spaced shallow furrows with diagonal ridges here and there.

The tree may grow from 5-20 meters tall (15-60'), typically with a thick, conical, fairly short, straight trunk .5-1.5 meters in diameter. Western Juniper often develops many large branches, even low down and frequently the main trunk divides into 2 or 3 forks, producing a wide topped tree. Some branches may be long and spreading, others short and stubby, but both types usually are dense.

The small round (.5-1 cm) berry is deep blue or blue-black under its white "bloom," and is resinous and quite dry. The skin is tough

and the scale tips are quite inconspicuous. The berries mature by the fall of the second year but stay on the tree all winter.

Because this species often grows on rocky exposed slopes or ledges, it is frequently seen as a large, fantastically twisted, picturesque tree with huge roots disappearing into rock cracks. They produce tremendous root systems in any situation, which of course makes it possible for them to survive in high windswept areas and amazingly arid regions as in eastern Oregon and Washington. They may be found in the rocky habitat there bordering sagebrush areas.

Western Juniper may occur in scattered pure stands or along with Jeffrey and Lodgepole Pines. It always grows where it gets full sun.

Usually, this is a tree of high windswept slopes, flats or rocky regions, occurring as low as 3,000 feet elevation in the north or as high as 10,500 feet in the south. It is common in the Sierra Nevada, especially on the eastern slopes, from southern California north to Oregon, Washington and southern British Columbia, and into drier portions of Idaho, Montana and western Nevada.

CALIFORNIA JUNIPER
(California Cedar)
Juniperus californica

This dry area juniper of California is very similar to the more widely distributed Western Juniper *(J. occidentalis)*, but grows at a much lower altitude. One distinctive characteristic is the trunk which is fluted and infolded far more than the Western Juniper which has widely spaced furrows. The bark is also very different— the surface bark may be quite grayish, but is red-brown underneath—not at all like the light cinnamon of the Western Juniper. The branchlets produce thin, scaly, ashy bark, not reddish as in the other species.

It usually is a much-branched shrub or small tree 1.5-4 meters tall, producing a rounded but fairly open-crowned tree, though it also may grow in a conical form to 11 meters.

The blunt-tipped, tiny, scale leaves are closely attached in 3's along the round twig. Each scale has a pit on the back and are definitely yellow-green in color. Young shoots may have a few sharp-pointed spreading leaves at the tip. The wood is very similar to Western Juniper. The fruit is definitely reddish when ripe, with a paper-thin skin; the whole berry is round, quite smooth and rather biggish for a juniper.

It is mainly a central to southern California tree, extending into Baja California. It grows from Mt. Diablo in the inner Coast

Ranges south to the Tehachapi Mountains and the desert slopes of the San Gabriel and San Bernadino Mountains, and also in the dry western Sierra foothills south from Kern River. It is generally found on dry slopes and flats at 2,000–4,000 feet elevation along with Piñon Pine, and in desert areas with Joshua Trees.

ROCKY MOUNTAIN JUNIPER
(Rocky Mountain Red Cedar)
Juniperus scopulorum

Usually this is a short-trunked tree, 5-7 meters tall and 15-25 cm in diameter, with a narrow rounded crown with many large branches. Multiple trunks from the ground are also a common form, but in canyon areas it usually is a single-trunked, fairly slender tree and develops drooping branches. These drooping branches (or at least drooping branch *tips*) are *the* distinguishing characteristic; otherwise it looks very much like the Utah Juniper.

The tiny leaves on the twigs are minute, sharp-pointed scales; on the squarish branchlets they are much longer and the sharp points tend to "stick out," developing a 4-row pattern. The leaves are green, but because of a whitish bloom the tree appears grayish or even bluish.

The thin-skinned oval berries take two years to mature; they are really blackish but appear medium blue in color because of their natural bloom. The pulp is sweet but resinous.

This juniper grows very slowly, usually on dry exposed mesas and mountain slopes, but larger in canyon bottoms. It is found with Mountain Mahogany and Piñon Pine and Utah Juniper in much of its range. It grows from the eastern foothills of the Rocky

Mountains in Alberta, south to Texas, but it is also found in scattered areas in the Northwest, south from British Columbia to eastern Oregon (mainly east of the Cascades) to Nevada and northern Arizona.

ONE-SEED JUNIPER
(New Mexico Cedar, Cherry-stone Juniper)
Juniperus monosperma

This is a very common juniper of the southwest, tending to be shrubby or just a small tree with many trunks from the root crown. It is usually seen as a conical shape, dotting the reddish slopes. It is very similar to the Utah Juniper in foliage, but that species is usually tree-like with one distinctive trunk (though its branching may be low). More importantly, the One-seeded Juniper can readily be distinguished by its very small berries. They are .5 cm or less in diameter while the berries of the Utah Juniper are from .5 to 1.2 cm in diameter. The twigs of the One-seed Juniper tend to be reddish brown while the Utah Juniper has greenish twigs.

The scale-like leaves, in alternate pairs, are yellowish-green, pointed at the tip but rounded on the back and fringed at the edge with minute teeth (use hand lens).

The small berries only have one seed. They may be copper color, though usually are quite bluish with their persistent bloom; they are thin-fleshed but moist.

This juniper prefers drier areas than the Rocky Mountain Juniper. It is usually found growing with the Piñon Pine *(P. edulis)*. It grows on mountain slopes and mesas from southeastern Nevada, southern Utah and southern Colorado, practically throughout New Mexico and Arizona (except the western edge), and south into Mexico. It has spread from its natural habitat following overgrazing.

ALLIGATOR JUNIPER
(Tascate)
Juniperus deppeana

The Alligator Juniper is often a beautiful big tree with wide-spreading branches and a large, thick-barked trunk checkered in an unusual pattern of dark reddish-brown squarish plates—hence the common name of Alligator Juniper. Although the scale-like leaves are very similar to Utah Juniper *(J. oesteosperma)* and the One-seed Juniper *(J. monosperma)*, the bark is so characteristic that it separates it from those junipers immediately. Once seen, it is a characteristic that won't be forgotten, and this bark develops even on young specimens.

It tends to be a wide tree rather than a tall tree, but it may grow to be as much as 20 meters (60') tall, the heavy trunk is 1.3-2 meters (4-6') in diameter. If the tree is cut, it often sprouts from the remaining trunk.

The fruit is the dry berry that is characteristic of junipers—reddish brown with a whitish bloom which usually disappears fairly early. The berries are quite large—definitely larger than the One-seeded Juniper of course, but tending to be bigger and much more red-brown than the Utah Juniper.

Found in the mountains of central and southeastern Arizona, central and southwestern New Mexico, western Texas, and south into Mexico. It is a truly magnificent and unusual juniper.

DWARF JUNIPER
(Common Juniper)
Juniperus communis

This is the only juniper having needle-like rather than scale-like leaves. The dark green, shiny, sharp needles are small, rigid, arranged in whorls of three, and are jointed at the base so they do not lie tightly along the branch. The needles are convex on the lower surface and have a noticeable white band of stomates down the length. Dwarf Juniper is an excellent common name, for only in a very few places does it grow taller than two meters. Mostly it spreads sideways, often covering areas ten meters across. The bark is chocolate brown, with thin, loose scales.

The berries are almost black with a whitish "bloom" when they mature at the end of the second season. Three points (actually the tips of the scales) stick out at the top of the small oval berry.

The wood is pale yellow-brown, heavy, fine-grained, tough, and very durable. Dwarf Juniper provides excellent ground cover because of the mat of growth it produces. It grows on stony or wooded slopes, with Lodgepole Pine, Douglas Fir, Yellow Pine, and various spruces from sea level in the Arctic to 11,000 feet in the Rockies and the Sierra Nevada.

It is found in western North America from Alaska south to Mono Pass in the Sierra Nevada, through the Rockies to Texas, New Mexico, and Arizona. In the east it extends south from Greenland along the Appalachians to northern Georgia, Ohio, Michigan and Nebraska. It is found all across northern Eurasia.

WESTERN YEW
Taxus brevifolia

Western Yew is easily recognized by its *dark* green, 2-ranked needles with a sharp (but not stiff) point, and the definite ridge down the center of the upper surface. The fruit, when present, is also very distinctive, for it is an orange or salmon-colored cup-shaped "berry"—not at all like the cones found on most conifers. However, the male and female trees are separate, so you'll only find this fruit on the female trees. It develops on the underside of the twig.

The foliage is deep, deep shiny green, especially in contrast to the brilliant green of young growth. The needle has a definite stalk which runs down the twig a bit—these stalks give the twig a linear, scale-like, rough appearance, but do not form a "peg" as do

spruces. The lower surface of the leaf is paler and the edges are slightly rolled under.

May grow to be 25 meters tall (75') in coastal areas of Washington, but it is never a common tree. The tree is slender with branches of unequal length, tending to sweep downwards.

The bark is thin and the papery reddish-purple scales keep peeling, showing a rosy under layer. The lower portion of the mature tree trunk is fluted.

The Western Yew grows best in coastal areas. It is found from British Columbia south through coastal parts of the Olympics and the Coast Ranges of Oregon and California to just south of San Francisco; also in the Cascades of Washington, Oregon and the Sierra Nevada up to 8,000 feet, in the Blue Mountains of Oregon and east to the Rocky Mountains of Idaho and Montana.

CALIFORNIA NUTMEG
(Stinking Yew)
Torreya californica

The California Nutmeg is a beautiful dark green tree, 5-18 meters (15-50') tall and seldom more than 60 cm (2') in diameter. The trees grow very slowly, and a "small" tree may be a hundred years old. The bark is thin and quite smooth. The most characteristic feature is the very sharp prickle at the tip of each needle. The needles are flat, 2.5-4.5 cm (1-1.75'') long, with two grooves running along their length. They are .3 cm wide at the bottom, .1 cm just at the tip before the tannish colored prickle. The petioles twist so that the needles stand out horizontally from the branch, making a flat spray. A Nutmeg might be confused with Douglas Fir, but if the needles are touched, you will immediately be aware of the main difference. The branches, like the needles, tend to be arranged in opposite pairs from the main branch. When the leaves are crushed, they give off a somewhat peculiar odor, giving it another common name—Stinking Yew.

The common name of "nutmeg" was given because its fruit resembles the tropical spice, nutmeg, but there is no relationship. The cone is not like the woody cones found on most conifers, but looks like a blue-green olive or plum, 2.5-4 cm long (1-1.75''). The seeds are big and were roasted and eaten by Indians. Only female trees will have the fruit, for the sexes are separate in this species. Mature trees not having the fruit are the male trees, which produce many tiny hanging pollen sacs.

This tree tends to be "shy" and grows in scattered small stands, often just one tree in a spot, never in groves. Found in between 100–6,000 feet elevation depending on latitude in the California Coast Ranges as far north as southern Mendocino County and south to the Santa Cruz Mountains. In the Sierra it is found on the western slope from Tehama County to Tulare County. It is always fun to find, and it is easy to recognize by the flat, sharp-tipped needles. Some that are easy to see are located just above El Portal going into Yosemite National Park.

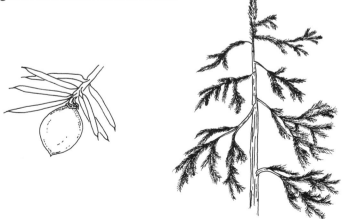

Chapter IV

CALIFORNIA PALM AND JOSHUA

JOSHUA TREE
Yucca brevifolia

The Joshua is a yucca that is really "tree-like," with huge branching arms, each ending in a large cluster of long, narrow, pointed, sharp leaves. Below the cluster the dead leaves hang mainly downwards, thickly covering the large limbs for some distance and making them look as though they are shaggy with coarse hair. Below a certain point, the old leaves fall off, leaving low, curving, ridge scars. The main trunk, and sometimes the lowest part of the larger branches, develops shallow vertical grooves with horizontal cross checks, giving a squarish pattern.

Young trees do not branch until they bloom. When they are about three or four meters tall (9-12'), they send up a flower stalk. After it withers, a side branch develops below the tip; in this way the paired branch structure develops. This pattern is continued, with the branches often developing at right angles, so a wide-crowned tree is produced. The silhouette is very recognizable with this regular branching and the thick-set branches with closely drooping dead leaves—often extending ten feet down the branch. The Joshua tree is frequently 5-10 meters tall (15-30'), and one half to one meter in diameter.

The leaves are 15-30 cm long (6-12"), narrow (1.5 cm), straight, tapering gradually from the base to the reddish or brown sharp point. The upper surface of the leaf is flat or concave, the lower surface convex or keeled, and the edges have tiny teeth.

The greenish white flowers have three thick sepals and three thick petals very much alike. The flowers are arranged in a branching cluster 20-35 cm from the ends of branches. The six-celled capsule matures in June. It is a large, spongy fruit 6-10 cm long, 4-5 cm wide, filled with flat black seeds.

The wood is soft but fibrous; it was tried for wood pulp, but didn't prove satisfactory. Joshua Trees grow, often abundantly, on desert slopes and mountain talus in sandy or gravelly soil. It is to be found with California Juniper and Piñon Pine or may grow in pure stands in higher elevations. It usually ranges between 2,000 and

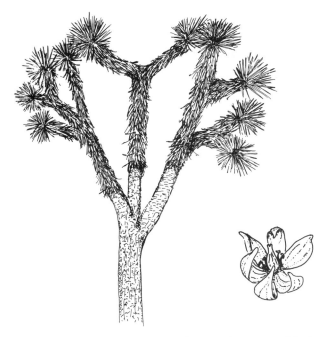

6,500 feet elevation, and grows in southwestern Utah, eastern
Arizona, southern Nevada and on the edges of California deserts.

DESERT PALM
(California Fan Palm)
Washingtonia filifera

The California Fan Palm is found naturally in scattered groups
in canyons on the eastern side of the desert mountains of southern
California, western and northern edges of the Colorado Desert and
the Mohave Desert, Baja California and canyons above Yuma,
Arizona. Palm Springs and Twenty-Nine Palms are famous localities for these limited-area natives, though the Twenty-Nine Palms
grove may have been one planted by the Indians long ago. They are
found on or near the old beach line of the ancient inland sea that
occupied that area. They are, however, commonly seen now in any
warm place where they can grow, especially seen in Florida, California, Hawaii, and along the Riviera. They were first discovered
by the Franciscan Fathers (in Baja California) as they made their
way north. The type specimen was even described from a tree
planted in Europe!

This palm is easily recognized by the large fan-shaped leaves, 1.5-2 meters (4-6') long, on equally long flat stems. The leaf is actually fan-folded, with forty to sixty alternating folds, each splitting deeply and ending in long slender drooping fibers. The stem has stout, recurving flattened spines on the edges. Many leaves fan out from the trunk-top, the upper ones vertical, the lower ones successively more horizontal, and as they begin to wither, they hang down, thickly covering the top portion of the trunk; unless removed, they often cover the whole trunk like a thatch. These were used by the Indians to thatch their shelters, and the leaf fibers, of course, were used in basketry.

Under the leaves the trunk appears pebbly-smooth, with circular markings. The California Fan Palm may grow to be 10-35 meters (30-90') tall, with the trunk half a meter to a meter in diameter (18-38").

The long, branching, flowering stalk grows from the axils of the upper leaves and has many tiny cream-colored flowers, each developing into a black, oval berry with the large seed covered by dry, thin flesh. The berries are edible; the Indians ground the seeds into flour.

Chapter V

BROADLEAF TREES

CALIFORNIA BLACK WALNUT
Juglans californica
Juglans hindsii

The California Black Walnut is usually a low, wide-crowned tree 4-10 meters high (12-30'), though it may grow as tall as 18 meters. The trunk is short, often forked near the base, with big upward-trending branches with drooping tips. The trunk of old trees is very roughly fissured with narrow, deep furrows and ridges very dark in color. The young trees and branches are a smooth steel gray. It resembles the eastern species very much.

The leaves are pinnately compound from 9-17 small toothed leaflets each 2.6-6 cm long, and the whole leaf being 15-20 cm long (6-9'').

It produces a very hard small nut which does not break open by itself, surrounded by a firm, pulpy, persistent covering which stains hands and clothing but also is useful as a dye. The male and female flowers are separate but on the same tree. They appear after the leaves have unfolded. The male is a many-stamened catkin, developing from last season's growth. The female flowers are in small clusters at the tip of this season's growth—at first they are small, green, and vase-shaped with 2 yellow stigmas, later developing into hard-shelled nuts 2-3 cm (¾-1.5'') in the fall. The thin brown husk eventually breaks off.

It is found along stream borders and moist gravelly ravines similar to situations where Sycamores grow, in the foothills and valleys of coastal southern California, particularly 20 or 30 miles inland.

Juglans hindsii is the northern California species and was probably brought to northern California by the Indians, for they are found most commonly growing around old Indian sites. The Northern California Black Walnut tends to have a straight single trunk. The leaves usually have more leaflets (15-19) and each leaflet is bigger, 5-10 cm long (2-4''), and the whole leaf is 24-30 cm (9-12''). The nuts are also larger, but not as large as the Eastern Black Walnut. This northern species is found mainly around the lower Sacramento River and the area around Walnut Creek,

though it is widely used as a street and city tree. The northern species is extensively used as the roots for English Walnuts which are grafted to the native species since it is more immune to diseases.

ARIZONA WALNUT
(Nogal)
Juglans major

The town of Nogales was named for the ''nogals'' growing in the canyonlands and washes in the area. This Nogal or Arizona Walnut is easily recognized as a Black Walnut with its yellowish-green pinnately compound leaves, the dark bark, and the hard small nut.

It is very common; in a good location may grow to be a tree 12-16 or more meters tall (36-50'). Like the California Walnut it tends to develop low branches or it may be many-trunked. In moist spots it will grow as a single straight tall trunk. The branches and young trunks are smooth and grayish, but the bigger branches and the main trunk soon develop deep grooves, the bark thickens, and becomes charcoal brown.

The pinnately compound leaf usually will have 9-13 leaflets, with the ones at the base smaller than the others. They are finely serrate, fairly long pointed and yellowish-green in color.

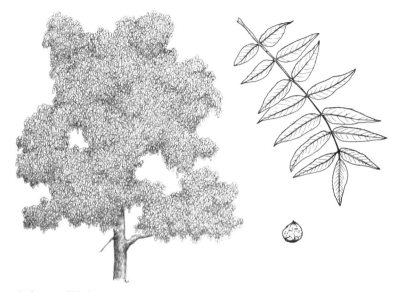

Arizona Walnut is found in canyons and along streams in the mountains and foothills from south central Colorado and north central Arizona (near Flagstaff) to southeastern Arizona, western New Mexico, and south to the mountains of northern Mexico. It will grow in areas too dry for alders, ashes, and cottonwoods.

WAX MYRTLE
(California Bayberry)
Myrica californica

The Wax Myrtle is a small evergreen tree that has peculiarly rough old branch stems, for when the leaves fall, raised leaf scars remain on the old twigs. The bark is smooth, light gray-brown with the inner bark dark red; tan-gray on branches. There are many branches, most of them very crooked and often there will be many trunks from the base. This small tree seems almost a black-green in color from a distance, for it is so dark. The undersides of the leaves

Wax Myrtle is generally found in sandy areas near the ocean or in other soils, including boggy areas, back from the sea, on hills and long streams, but usually not inland more than ten miles or so. Found from northern Washington to southern California.

The very dark, glossy, green, narrow leaves are 5-10 cm long (2-4''), somewhat convex on the upper surface. The undersurface has many minute glands and the slightly toothed margin tends to

roll under. The leaves are clustered at the ends of long, thin, branches.

The female catkins are in the upper leaf axils (back from the tip a ways), the flowers with bright red-purple styles and green bumpy ovaries. There is also a group of mixed male and female flowers in catkins somewhat lower. Near the base of the leafy twig will be male catkins, the flowers with dark purple anthers and bright yellow pollen. The fruit is a dry drupe, with many crowded together. They are warty, dark purple and covered with a gray wax. In the fall these abundant, dark, crowded fruits near the branch tips make the Wax Myrtle particularly noticeable.

ASPENS, POPLARS, COTTONWOODS
Populus

Key to Species of Populus

1 a. Tall, slender tree, all branches ascending
        close to trunk—Lombardy Poplar, *Populus
        nigra*, See Intruders . . .   turn to page 193

   b. Tree not slender, branching outwards (and
        then perhaps upwards), making rounded or
        irregular silhouette not narrow or slender
        . . .   go to #2

2   a.   Leaf petioles flattened from side to side; leaves roundish or triangular . . .   go to #3

      b.   Leaf petioles round, though may taper, *not* flattened from side to side; leaves longer than wide . . .   go to #4

3   a.   Leaves almost round, usually 6 cm or less across—Aspen, *Populus tremuloides* . . .   turn to page 102

      b.   Leaves triangular, usually wider than 6 cm . . .   go to #5

4   a.   Leaves willow-like, 5 to 6 times as long as wide—Narrowleaf Poplar, *Populus angustifolia* . . .   turn to page 107

      b.   Leaves broader . . .   go to #6

5   a.   Very squat triangular leaf wider than long; margin toothed; frequent in western states—Fremont Cottonwood, *Populus fremontii* . . .   turn to page 103

      b.   Triangular leaf; margin more toothed; mainly in plains states and into eastern Rockies—Plains or Sargent's Cottonwood, *Populus sargentii* . . .   turn to page 106

6   a.   Leaves lance-shape, almost twice as long as wide—Lance-leaf Cottonwood, *Populus acuminata* . . .   turn to page 108

      b.   Leaves oval, about 1½ times as long as wide . . .   go to #7

7   a.   Exceptionally long leaf petiole; leaves oval; rusty or brownish undersurface (or pale); very long winter buds, with yellow balsam fluid; scattered in the west; mainly found in eastern states, Canada and northern states—Balsam Poplar, *Populus balsamifera* . . .   turn to page 106

      b.   Leaves broad, oval; pale underneath; winter buds resinous; abundant throughout west—Black Cottonwood, *Populus trichocarpa* . . .turn to page 104

QUAKING ASPEN
Populus tremuloides

A beautiful tree and amazingly enough, it is the most widespread tree of the western hemisphere. A very similar species is just as extensive in Eurasia. Both species grow from the Arctic tundra regions at practically sea level to high in the mountains in middle latitudes. In our hemisphere it grows from southern Labrador to Hudson Bay, west to Alaska, spreading south through western Canada and the mountains of western United States into New Mexico and Arizona, and even high in the mountains of Baja California and Mexico. It also grows in the east.

The aspen is the most conspicuous deciduous mountain tree, noticeable immediately because the round ovate leaves always seem to be moving, even in the lightest breezes. It grows as a stunted tree in the Arctic regions or the alpine regions of high mountains, but in prime locations it is a beautiful straight tree with smooth whitish bark, only roughened and thickened near the base. Many black, rounded or curved bumps and branch scars irregularly mark the white bark, making the tree stand out whether in grassy groves or mixed with conifers in open woods. Sometimes the trunk will have pale yellow or greenish areas.

The tree is usually slender, seldom more than 35 cm (14'') in diameter and 10-15 meters (30-40') tall. However, mature stands may have trees up to 27 meters (80') tall and may be 60 cm in diam-

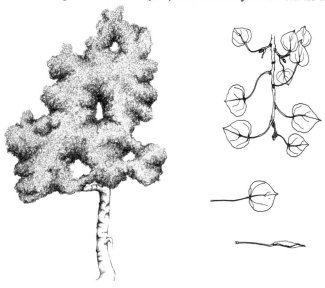

eter. The trunk often is clear of low branches. The branches "prune themselves"—i.e. drop off as they are replaced by higher ones as the tree grows. It may take a while for the dead branches to drop off, so usually the lowest branch or two is dead and will be amazingly dry even in hard rains or wet snows, so it is a good tree for firewood when these conditions catch you when camping or hiking. The branches break easily if dry; if they aren't dry, they aren't dead.

The leaves "quake" because the petiole is not only long but also it is flattened at right angles to the surface of the leaf; this allows maximum pivoting at their joining. The leaves are smooth and shiny both top and bottom, the upper surface deep yellowish-green (or bluish-green in some localities), paler underneath, and smooth. They are one of the fabulous color-producers in the fall.

Aspens are found mostly on moist slopes and in canyons with well-drained soils. They grow mainly in the Canadian Zone along with Red Fir, Mountain Hemlock, Lodgepole Pine, Engelmann, White, Blue, and Black Spruces, and White Fir. In the far north and in high mountain spots they may make pure stands.

FREMONT COTTONWOOD
(Alamo Gila Cottonwood)
Populus fremontii

Cottonwoods were one of the favorite trees of the westward pioneers, for the sight of them always meant water, wood, and shade. Fremont Cottonwood looks very like the common cottonwood of the east and midwest *(Populus deltoides)* and the cottonwood of central New Mexico, Texas, and the Rio Grande *(Populus wislizenii)*.

Fremont Cottonwood is usually from 20-35 meters tall (60-110'), with a trunk which may grow to be 1.5 meters (4.5') in diameter. The trunk generally leans or is bent and the first branches are often about half way up. The main branches are normally thick, spreading, and drooping. The bark on the lower trunk is light gray-brown and deeply furrowed with rough ridges. Bark on large branches is only slightly ridged and is ashy brown.

The winter buds are 4 mm long, sharp-pointed with light green scales. The leathery leaves are 4-7 cm long (1½-2½"), triangular-shape, smooth and yellow-green on both sides. They turn clear yellow in the fall. One very basic characteristic is the petiole, which is flattened from side to side (at right angles to the flat blade of the leaf). This enables any breeze to set the leaf in motion.

The male flower is a long catkin crowded with stamens with dark red anthers. The female flower, also in a catkin, develops into a string of capsules like angular beads, each holding many tiny seeds in a thick tuft of white cottony hairs. This is so abundant that it literally carpets an area with white cotton.

Grows along stream banks, damp valley floors and low hills of central and southern California in the low elevations of both the Coast Ranges and the Sierra, to Baja California, through central Nevada, southern Utah, northern Arizona and northwestern New Mexico. This is *the* cottonwood along the Colorado River in the Grand Canyon. It is frequently planted as a shade tree, especially in the southwest and Mexico.

BLACK COTTONWOOD
Populus trichocarpa

Black Cottonwood is the largest cottonwood; in fact, it is the tallest-growing deciduous tree in the west. May grow to 60 meters (180') and old ones become nearly 3 meters in diameter (9'), though generally it is 25-40 meters (75-100').

It is quite easily recognized even from a distance, especially if a breeze is blowing, for the whitish underside is very noticeable as the leaves flip—whereas the Fremont Cottonwood is green (and usually a yellowish-green) on *both* sides. Close up, the Black Cottonwood

can also be distinguished by its *round* petioles (not flattened side-ways) and its leaf shape, which is less triangular than the Fremont Cottonwood. The bulge comes one-third of the way up the leaf, not almost at its connection to the petiole as in Fremont Cottonwood. Black Cottonwood tapers from that mid-bulge to its sharp apex. The young leaves may be fairly narrow and finely toothed. The leaves are thick, 5-8 cm long (2-3''). They are more or less hairy when young, but become smooth and deep shiny green above, the rusty veins showing against the dull whitish underneath.

Usually there are no branches for half the height of the tree and the branches likewise tend to have no side branches for half their length. The bark is gray, ashy-gray on the mature trunks, with thick, regular and deep furrows. The winter buds are resinous and long-pointed, often curving, the terminal one 2 cm long.

The male flowers are in long catkins with many stamens. The female flowers mature into angled capsules holding many cottony-tufted small seeds which, when ripe, float through the air and drift into deep piles.

Black Cottonwood is a common tree, found on stream banks and in valleys from southern Alaska, south to southern California, and east to northern Idaho.

BALSAM POPLAR
(Tacamahac)
Populus balsamifera

The Balsam Poplar is the most common poplar (cottonwood) of the northern parts of North America—from Alaska, across Canada and into the north central and northeastern states. It is only found in scattered areas of the northwestern states of Idaho, Montana, Wyoming, and North Dakota.

It has exceptionally long leaf stems and the leaves are narrower than the Black Cottonwood *(P. trichocarpa)* which it resembles, since its leaves are also shiny above and pale beneath. The Balsam Poplar, however, has brownish or rusty undersides, not just paler green. The thin but leathery leaves are sharp pointed, usually slightly rounded at the base and have a finely notched margin. The slender stem is long (2.5-5 cm) and is round. The branches are stout and erect, and its silhouette is much narrower than Black Cottonwood.

The tree grows to 25-30 meters (75-90') tall, and old trees may be quite thick trunked, 1.5-2 meters (4-6') in diameter. Usually there are no branches for the first ten meters or so (30'). Young trees have a smooth, brownish or greenish bark, but old trees develop thick, somewhat reddish-gray bark which is regularly and deeply grooved between the thick broad ridges.

SARGENT'S COTTONWOOD
(Plains Cottonwood)
Populus sargentii

This is *the* common cottonwood of the plains, coming into the west in the eastern Rockies from Alberta south into northeastern New Mexico. The leaf is similar to Fremont Cottonwood *(P. fremontii)* in its triangular shape, but it has a more noticeably toothed margin and is usually wider (7 cm) than long (6 cm), while the Fremont Cottonwood tends to have an even more squat shape.

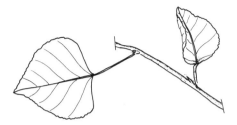

The stem is flattened, with small glands at the base of the blade. The bark on young trees or upper branches of old trees is a smooth whitish green. The mature tree has rough, light gray, deeply furrowed bark with broad ridges. The tree may grow to be 30 meters (90') tall, though usually only 18-25 meters (50-75'), and often up to 1.3 meters in diameter (4').

NARROWLEAF COTTONWOOD
Populus angustifolia

The Narrowleaf Cottonwood is well-named, for its leaves are not the typical triangular shape you think of in connection with cottonwoods. In fact, the leaves are long and narrow—5-7 cm long, 1.5 cm wide (2-3'' long, ¾'' wide)—very willow-like in shape. This tree, however, grows tall and slender, and the young bark and branches are very whitish, not like willows. The leaves are finely serrated, sticky on the underside.

The next year's leaf buds are brown and shiny and ooze a yellowish sticky substance when touched. The mature bark is gray and furrowed, though not as deeply as other cottonwoods.

The Narrowleaf Cottonwood grows along streams or in moist areas, often at higher elevations than its relatives, and is commonly found with Yellow Pines *(P. ponderosa)*. It is found in Utah, Colorado, abundantly in most of Arizona except the southwestern portion, south into Mexico.

LANCE-LEAF COTTONWOOD
Populus acuminata

This cottonwood is sometimes considered a cross between Sargent's and Narrowleaf Cottonwood, but it is most often found in areas far from Sargent's Cottonwood. All of these trees are very similar in their growth habits, but the leaf shapes are dissimilar.

The Lance-leaf is wider than the slender leaf of the Narrowleaf, but not as wide as the Sargent's triangular one. It is also a much shorter leaf. The bark on young trees is almost as white as on the Narrowleaf Cottonwood. This cottonwood is found in central Arizona, and extends into the edge of New Mexico, southeastern Utah and southern Colorado. The young buds tend to be greenish.

WILLOWS

Key to Species of Willows

1 a.   Leaves smooth-margined, widest above the
            middle . . .   go to #2

     b.   Leaves finely serrated . . .   go to #3

2 a.   Leaves shiny dark green above, whitish or
            grayish on underside; edge rolled; very common in the west—Arroyo Willow, *Salix lasiolepis* . . .   turn to page 109

     b.   Leaves lustrous yellow-green above; whitish, hairy underneath—River Willow, *Salix scouleriana* . . .   turn to page 111

3 a.   Mature leaves usually broad (3 cm) and long; widest *below* the middle . . .   ❜go to #4

     b.   Mature leaves more slender; usually not more than 2 cm wide . . .   go to #5

4 a.   Small wart-like glands on petiole at base of blade; large round stipules; long pointed leaves—Yellow Willow, *Salix lasiandra* . . . **turn to page 111**

   b.   Conspicuous yellow midveins; small stipules; red, smooth twigs—Red Willow, *Salix laevigata* . . . **turn to page 110**

5 a.   Twigs separate easily from branch, not tearing. Leaves often sickle-shaped, gray-green—Gooddings Willow, *Salix gooddingii* . . . **turn to page 112**

   b.   Yellow branchlets droop, giving weeping effect; pale green shiny leaves—Peach Leaf Willow, *Salix amygdaloides* . . . **turn to page 113**

ARROYO WILLOW
Salix lasiolepis

This willow is one of the very common stream bank trees of the west. It may be a shrub or up to 13 meters tall (36'). Generally it produces many smallish trunks, which become irregularly broad ridged as they increase in size. The branchlets are smooth, brownish or greenish, and the twigs are yellowish or brownish.

The branches all trend upwards and tend to have groups of side branchlets growing from approximately the same place. This is particularly noticeable near the branch ends.

The leaves are between 4 and 10 cm long and 1-2 cm wide, definitely widest above the middle. The young shoots tend to have longer leaves. They are shiny dark green above and grayish underneath, but not noticeably hairy (at least when mature). The very edge is rolled under (use hand lens).

The Arroyo Willow grows up to 6,000 feet elevation, from eastern Washington, Oregon and Idaho to California, western Nevada, Arizona, and western New Mexico.

RED WILLOW
(Polished Willow, Smooth Willow)
Salix laevigata

This willow is a tree from 6-16 meters tall (18-48'). The scientific name means "smooth"—referring to the yellowish or red-brown very smooth twigs which tend to be slim. The bark of both trunks and big branches, however, is rough, furrowed, and dark brown. Usually it is quite a straight, unbranched trunk, with the slender branches producing a well-formed crown.

The leaves are very finely toothed, light shiny green above, whitish below, and pointed at the tip. They are 7-15 cm long, 1.5-3 cm wide, and are wider below or at the middle—somewhat like *Salix lasiandra*, but there are no wartish glands on the petioles. The stipules are small and may not even be present on the older stems, for they wither early. The leaves have conspicuous yellow mid-veins seen mostly on the upper surface.

The Red Willow is commonly found with many different plant groups along streams below 5,000 feet from northern California to Mexico, then east to southern Nevada, southern Utah, and western Arizona.

YELLOW WILLOW
(Western Black Willow)
Salix lasiandra

This willow usually grows 5-12 meters tall (15-36') but often it is taller and it may get to be more than 40 cm in diameter. The trunk tends to be short, crooked or leaning, but with long upright branches which produce an open, graceful crown. The large leaves give it a very different silhouette, even at a distance, from that of short-leaved species. The twigs are large, reddish or yellow-brown, shiny smooth.

The leaves are deep shiny yellow-green, resembling a peach leaf in shape and size. They are paler beneath and are silky-hairy when young, though this disappears as they mature. The round, prominent, paired stipules at the base of each leaf are especially noticeable on actively-growing twigs.

The distinctive characteristic of this willow is the presence of two or three dark, small, wart-like glands on each side of the petiole just where the leaf expands.

Found abundantly along streams, lakes and damp slopes in the west, often with alders, cottonwoods and sycamore. It is usually very noticeable because of its long pointed leaves. It apparently blooms later than many other willows, for the seed catkins remain on the branchlets when other species have shed theirs. It is found from Alaska through western British Columbia, Washington, Oregon, and in both the Coast Ranges and on the western slopes of the Sierra Nevada in California and east to Idaho, Utah, Colorado and to northern New Mexico and Arizona. It grows from sea level to 7,000 feet elevation.

RIVER WILLOW
(Scoulers Willow, Fire Willow)
Salix scouleriana

River Willow may be found as a shrub, especially in its northern range, but normally it is a tree up to 10 meters (30') tall. The thick firm leaves tend to be variable in size and shape, but they are smooth-margined, usually yellow-green, lustrous on the upper surface, but definitely whitish on the lower surface. They are at least somewhat hairy, or may be densely hairy. They will be from 5-10 cm long and 1.5-3 cm wide, widest above the middle and coming to the tip abruptly. Stipules may be ear-shaped and quite large or they may be small, and will only be on the new year's growth. The midveins are yellow, the side veins quite inconspicuous.

The twigs are stout, the young ones yellowish, the older ones very dark red-brown. The lower trunk will be wide-ridged, dark blackish-brown with a reddish cast.

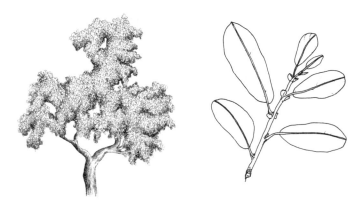

The common name of Fire Willow is given because this species is one of the first to come in after a disaster.

It is probably the most common willow growing in moist woods, brushy slopes and along streams up to 10,000 feet. It grows with many different plant groups, but always where there is moisture, but not necessarily running or standing water. It is found from Alaska down the coast of British Columbia, Washington, Oregon and California. It is also common in the Sierra Nevada, and east into the Rocky Mountains, especially Montana and Utah, then south to Arizona and New Mexico.

BLACK WILLOW
(Gooddings Willow, Valley Willow)
Salix gooddingii (nigra)

Many of the willows are commonly called "Black Willow" because the mature trunk is so often dark. Valley Willow is a better name for this willow though its trunk is dark, for it likes to grow along rivers, rather than just streams or by ponds. It is truly a tree willow, from 7-18 meters (20-55') tall. Often the trunk is forked from the base, with two or more main trunks so the branches make an irregular crown. The bark is very dark and roughly fissured. The twigs are yellowish and separate easily and cleanly.

The mature leaves are narrow, long-pointed, often sickle-shaped, and green with a "bloom" on both surfaces so they appear grayish-green; the young leaves are often hairy. They may be quite long, 5-17 cm (2-7''), but narrow. The stipules are fairly large, glandular on their upper surface, but they fall off very early.

Grows on river banks of the central valley of California, also in the lower hills of the southern Sierra and into Mexico, then east to Texas, mostly below 2,000 feet.

PEACH LEAF WILLOW
Salix amygdaloides

This willow has leaves very like a long, narrow peach, hence its most common name. It is the willow most often seen in the Rocky Mountains, occurring as far south as southern Utah and northwestern Arizona. It is also in eastern Washington and southern Oregon. It is widely distributed from British Columbia, east to Michigan and south in the plains states.

It may grow to be a big tree, 20 meters or so (60'). The trunk may become large, the big branches straight and erect, but the yellow branchlets droop.

The pale green shining leaves are up to 13 cm long (5''), with a long, tapering tip; the underside has a whitish bloom. The mid-rib is noticeably big and yellow or orangish.

PAPER BIRCH
Betula papyrifera

The Paper Birch grows to be a beautiful big tree up to 40 meters (120') with whitish and gray-brown or gray-reddish bark with horizontal marks and loose pieces that easily pull off. The inner bark is orange-brown. The base of the mature trees becomes very dark and somewhat roughened. The new twigs are hairy, with orange dots; older twigs are smooth reddish-bown.

The alternate, deciduous leaves are doubly serrate on slender petioles 6-10 cm long (2¼-4''). The seed catkins are 2.5-4 cm long, the middle lobe of the scale elongated. The male catkin is even longer.

The wood is very tough and fine-grained. The bark was used by the Indians for their canoes, which they sewed together with fibers from roots of the Larch. These Birch trees can be tapped for sugar,

as a Maple. If the bark is peeled, black scar tissue forms, so if you're looking for "paper" from a Paper Birch, don't peel it from a living tree. Paper Birch grows where it is moist and cool, preferring areas around mountain lakes, streams, and cool slopes. It is common and widespread in British Columbia, northern Alberta and east; south into northern Idaho and western Montana, and also in eastern Oregon. It is abundant on the coastal islands of western Canada.

WATER BIRCH
(Mountain Birch, Red Birch)
Betula occidentalis (fontinalis)

Water Birch (and many other common names for this lovely birch) is usually a many-trunked little birch that is always found in moist places, particularly along lively streams; it may grow as tall as 8 meters (25'). The trunk is very distinctive, partly because there are usually many of all sizes stemming from the base, but mostly because of its smooth, shiny red-bronze color and the fact that the bark does not peel. The young twigs are smooth and are peppered with many shiny yellow-green glands; older twigs are light bronze.

The leaves are oval-round, sharply toothed and are both glandular and finely hairy on the upper surface. They are alternately arranged, the lower leaves grouped closely on branchlets, often 2 or 3 at the tip of a short spur surrounding a bud.

The catkins are small, 2.5-3 cm, and are on slender stems.

Found in moist mountain areas, especially along rushing streams from 2,000–8,000 feet elevation in the Rocky Mountains from British Columbia to New Mexico and south from British Columbia to southern California in the mountains along the coast.

ALDERS

Alders may be tall trees, small trees, or even shrub-like, depending on the species and habitat. They produce male catkins and tiny female cones in separate clusters at twig tip at the end of the growing season, so they are noticeable if you look closely (especially for the tiny female cones) during the winter months when the tree is bare. Usually the catkins begin to open before the leaves unfurl, the male catkins shedding vast quantities of pollen, then drying and dropping off. The female cones gradually mature, the seeds ready by early fall. The leaves are usually double toothed or notched with very noticeable, almost parallel side veins.

WHITE ALDER
Alnus rhombifolia

White Alder is one of the common trees along streams and in canyon bottoms of the foothills and low mountains from British Columbia and northern Idaho into eastern Washington and Oregon, then south into both the Coast Ranges and western slopes of the Sierra Nevada to southern California. It often grows in thick groups, but intermixes with California Sycamore, Box-elder, Oregon Ash, etc.

It resembles the Red Alder, but this tree has thin, scaly, brown bark up the trunk quite a ways—Red Alder is much smoother. Also the margin of this leaf is not as deeply toothed.

White Alder generally grows straight and usually has no branches for half its height—which may be as much as 25 meters

(75'). The larger branches, also, often have no side branches for half of their length, giving the tree a very distinctive silhouette. The branches, especially the lower ones, droop at the ends. The diameter of the tree is usually between 45 and 60 cm. The twigs are reddish and smooth; the winter buds have fine hairy or downy scales.

The leaves are only slightly toothed and irregular, but the parallel side veins are noticeable. The lower leaf surface is fine-hairy.

The clustered male catkins are very long and since they open in late winter or early spring, they are very noticeable on the bare tree. Many small (1-1.5 cm) dark woody cones are produced.

RED ALDER
(Oregon Alder)
Alnus oregona

The Red Alder may be 15-25 meters tall (45-60'), or in poor locations it may even be shrub-like. It is largest in the Puget Sound area where it may be 20-30 meters tall.

The 6-12 cm long leaves are pointed at the tip, lobed or double toothed, but not as deeply as *Alnus sinuata*, woolly when young, dark green above, rust-hairy underneath, and the edge is rolled under.

The male catkins open to be 10-15 cm long, the cone usually only 2 or 2.5 cm long. The smooth bark is thin, very light gray, with reddish inner bark, only becoming slightly ridged in old trees. It is rough on the lower half of the tree, though this roughness does not extend as high as it does on the White Alder.

It grows on stream banks and marshes below 500 feet in mixed evergreen forests and redwood forests from Alaska south through British Columbia and its islands, western Washington and Oregon to the Santa Barbara area in southern California, on streams on the coastal side.

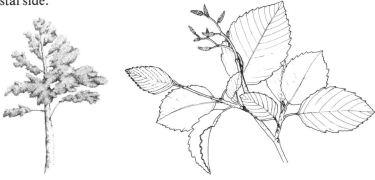

SITKA ALDER
Alnus sinuata (sitchensis)

In the north, the Sitka Alder may be a small tree (5-15 meters), but in the southern part of its range, it often grows only as a shrub. The bark is smooth and grayish, the twigs shiny but with light-colored specks.

When the leaves first open, they are sticky. As they expand they become shiny yellow-green above, and pale beneath with hairy veins. They are thin, pointed at the tip, double notched and 6-15 cm long.

The catkins open from May to July. The two to four clustered male catkins are 2.5-3 cm long, and the woody cone small, even when it matures (1.2-1.5 cm). They are produced on this season's growth, along with the leaves.

The Sitka Alder grows in wet places below 6,000 feet, down to sea level in the northern range. It is found from Alaska to northern California, and in the Rockies to Montana and Colorado.

MOUNTAIN ALDER
(Thin-leaf Alder)
Alnus tenuifolia

Mountain Alder often makes thickets along streams and in moist places at elevations of 4,000–8,000 feet. It may be shrub-like but often grows as tall as 4-6 meters (12-18'). The bark is smooth, usually reddish, but may be gray-brown. The roundish leaves are coarsely toothed and then serrated; they may be 3-6 cm long, are light green and thin in texture, usually fuzzy when young, becoming dark green above and yellow-green below as they mature.

Because of the altitude at which they grow, this alder doesn't open its brown male catkins (usually a cluster of 4 or 5 from a twig near the end of last season's growth) till April or May. They are about 2.5 cm long and are produced the previous fall and hang,

tightly closed through the winter. When they open, they may be as long as 7 cm. The female flowers are also produced in the fall and do not mature till late spring. They are tiny (.3-.5 cm), 3 or 4 of them on short stalks, stemming from a slender twig just back from the male blossoms. They develop into small woody cones.

The Mountain Alder grows from Alaska, south into the Rocky Mountains to New Mexico and through the Pacific states to the southern part of the Sierra Nevada. This is the common alder along streams, lakes and moist meadows of the eastern Cascades and Sierra Nevada, usually between 6,000 and 8,000 feet elevation along with Red Fir, Yellow Pine and Lodgepole Pine.

ARIZONA ALDER
(Mexican Alder)
Alnus oblongifolio

The Arizona Alder is very like the other alders except it grows in the desert regions; however, it must have cool canyons and running water.

The twigs become dark red-brown with very noticeable gray spots, the trunk is straight with smooth, thin, light gray-brown bark, sometimes tinged with red.

The leaves are dark yellow-green on the upper surface while underneath they are paler and have conspicuous scattered black glands.

The male flowers are noticeable because they appear early in the spring, before the leaves, as orange-brown catkins five or more centimeters long (2" +). The female flowers are tiny but have bright red stigmas. The oval woody cone that develops is 1-2.5 cm long.

It is usually found between 4,000 and 6,000 feet in the mountains or plateau areas around the Grand Canyon, central and southeastern Arizona, southwestern New Mexico and south into Mexico.

GIANT CHINQUAPIN
Castanopsis chrysophylla

The Giant Chinquapin is an easily recognized thick-barked evergreen tree 5-15 meters tall (15-45'), with small deep green leaves that are golden-hairy underneath. The young stems are also golden with hairs, the older branchlets very smooth.

It may grow to be a very large tree to 30 meters (90') with a diameter of one meter or more (3 + feet) in the Cascades of Oregon and the Coast Ranges of northern Californa. It ordinarily grows 5-15 meters tall.

The mature trunk has thick bark with long furrows. Young trees have dark gray, thin, smoothish bark.

The leathery leaves are smooth-margined, but often a bit wavy-edged, remaining on the tree for two to three years. Because the side twigs (which grow from the buds in the leaf axis) develop while those original leaves are still on the tree, there is usually a large leaf just below each side twig. The leaves are so dark green and heavy you can hardly see the veins on the top surface, but they are very noticeable on the golden underside. The veins tend to run quite regularly, and are parallel to each other.

The Giant Chinquapin grows abundantly on wooded slopes in moist areas from Washington in the Coast Ranges and the western side of the Cascades, south through Oregon and into Mendocino County in northern California. It is also common in the Sierra Nevada and Coast Ranges to mid-California, but generally south of Mendocino it is not as large.

TANBARK OAK
Lithocarpus densiflora

This near relative of the oaks was the main source of tannin for the leather industry in the west. It is an evergreen forest tree, growing 16-40 meters tall (50-100'), with thick gray-green bark with random cracks or furrows on the lower trunk, smooth gray above.

The leaves are very distinctive, for they are dark green above, with a grayish underside. There are prominent parallel side veins, each ending in a sharp tooth. The new leaves are reddish-gold, covered with white or reddish fuzz which mostly disappears, at least on the upper surfaces. The young branches are dense with short soft hair.

Many male flowers are crowded together in a smelly upright catkin (most catkins tend to hang) 6-10 cm long (2.5-4'') at branchlet ends. The female flowers are at the base of the male catkins or a short ways down the branchlet. They are much more noticeable than the tiny female flowers of the true oaks, and already they show the characteristic bristly cup, though at this stage the bristles are soft and green. The fruit is a thick-shelled acorn 2-3 cm long, sitting in a shallow bristly cup, soft felted inside.

It grows on wooded slopes of the Coast Ranges from southern Oregon to Ventura County in southern California, and on the western slope of the Sierra Nevada below 4,000 feet. Tanbark Oak grows most abundantly where there are redwoods.

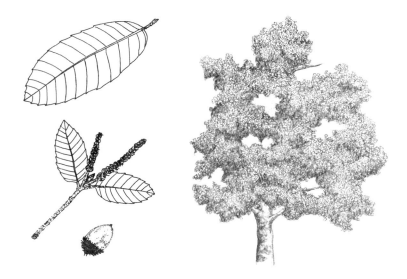

OAKS
Quercus

Oaks seem to have more numerous common names than any other group of trees—often with the same name applied in a different area to a very different oak—so, watch the scientific name carefully!

Oaks are broadleaf trees; some are evergreen, some are deciduous, all produce acorns. They tend to grow slowly, often to a large size, both in the main trunk and branches. They develop a long tap root very quickly. The wood is hard and the bark tends to be thick and often contains tannin. Most of them are big trees, but several Scrub Oaks are abundant, especially in the drier areas of the southwest.

The leaves may be evergreen, staying on the tree for 3 or 4 years, or only till the next spring or summer—or, they may be deciduous. They are always arranged alternately.

The male flowers are tiny, with many flowers hanging along dangling threads. The female flowers are tiny and are in axils of this season's new leaves. They look somewhat like leaf buds but there are stigmas out the top which are usually fuzzy. There may be one in an axil, or there may be a group of them. All oaks are wind pollinated. If the acorns mature in one season (the White Oak group), they will grow steadily after pollination. If they take two seasons to mature (the Black Oak group), they don't seem to do much growing until the second season.

The thin-shelled acorns always sit in cups, which vary greatly from one species to the next. White Oak acorns tend to be whitish, sweetish, and edible, while Black Oaks are darker and have more tannin, so they take some care (leaching with water) before they are pleasant to eat. The acorns are an important food for many birds and small mammals and many species were staples for the Indians. Oaks produce important commercial wood in the temperate regions worldwide.

The White Oaks tend to have light-colored wood and bark, and produce their acorns in one year. The Black Oaks tend to have dark bark, deeper-colored wood, and their acorns take two years to mature, have thin-scaled cups, and are fuzzy.

Key to Species of Oaks (Quercus)

1 a. Margin of leaf entire, serrate or spiny-toothed, but not jagged or lobed (or only a bit), evergreen, thickish leaves . . .   go to #2

   b. Margin of leaf lobed (shallow or deep), or jagged, jags may be bristle-tipped; deciduous; leaves thinnish . . .   go to #18

2 a. Margin (of at least some leaves, especially on older branches) *may* be entire (or only a small tooth near tip) . . .   go to #3

   b. Margins not entire; may be spiny, serrate, or toothed . . .   go to #7

3 a. Oaks only in the southwest (Arizona, New Mexico, Texas, Mexico generally). More or less scrubby, grayish leaves . . .   go to #4

   b. Oaks may be in southern Oregon, California, and the southwest; upper surface of leaf dark green; powdery yellow or powdery gray undersides—Canyon Live Oak, *Quercus chrysolepis* . . .   turn to page 134

   c. Oak only in California; upper leaf surface shiny dark green, under surface shiny yellow-green; no fuzz—Interior Live Oak, *Quercus wislizenii* . . .   turn to page 132

4 a. Acorns on long stalks (usually in 2's or 3's), noticeably raised veins—Net-leaf Oak, *Quercus reticulata* . . .   turn to page 141

   b. Acorns sessile or only short stalks . . .   go to #5

5 a. Undersurface with thick woolly hairs; shiny dark green upper surface; long, slender leaves with a small tooth or two near tip (sometimes)—Silver-leaf Oak, *Quercus hypoleucoides* . . .   turn to page 142

   b. Undersurface may be pale, but not thickly woolly . . .   go to #6

6 a. Twigs yellow and hairy; leaves oval—Gray
Oak, *Quercus grisea* . . .   turn to page 142

b. Usually tree-like; oblong leaves rusty bronze
in winter; cup with red-tipped coarse hairs;
leaves definitely blue-green—Mexican Blue
Oak, *Quercus oblongifolia* . . .   turn to page 143

7 a. Trees with leaf margins spiny, serrate, or
toothed (some leaves *may* be entire) . . .   go to #8

b. Scrub oaks, though may get to small
tree-size; with spiny, serrate or toothed
leaves . . .   go to #13

8 a. Trees with dark green leaves; upper surface
may be shiny or not; lower surface various
. . .   go to #9

b. Trees with gray-green or blue-green leaves;
found in southern California and the southwest . . .   go to #12

9 a. Leaves dark green on upper surface;
underside powdery yellow or powdery gray;
young leaves golden; hairy on underside—
Canyon Live Oak, *Quercus chrysolepis* . . .   turn to page 134

b. Leaves dark green on upper surface; not
yellow- or gray-powdery on underside . . .   go to #10

10 a. Leaves definitely convex; edges curled
under; teeth spine-tipped; underside may be
hairy at vein junctions or somewhat fuzzy—
Coast Live Oak, *Quercus agrifolia* . . .   turn to page 133

b. Leaves flat or flattish; teeth spiny or not . . . go to #11

11 a. Dark green upper surface; shiny yellow undersurface; *no* fuzz—Interior Live Oak, *Quercus wizlizenii* . . .   turn to page 132

    b. Very shiny on both surfaces; very flat leaf; two fuzzy spots at base of blade on underside—Emory Oak, *Quercus emoryii* . . .   turn to page 136

12 a. Lower surface of leaf with tan, thick, fine down; tree of Arizona, New Mexico, and Mexico—Arizona White Oak, *Quercus arizonica* . . .   turn to page 137

    b. Lower surface may be smooth or scattered hairy, paler than upper surface; found in southern California—Engelmann Oak, *Quercus engelmannii* . . .   turn to page 140

13 a. Scrub Oaks; acorn on *long* stalk; leaves almost smooth-margined; noticeable raised veins; found in southwest—Net-leaf Oak, *Quercus reticulata* . . .   turn to page 141

    b. Scrub oaks; acorns not on long stalks . . .   go to #14

14 a. Leaf small, holly-like, with spine-tipped teeth; not densely hairy or powdery below; flat or undulate leaves; not convex . . .   go to #15

    b. Leaf may be spiny but not regularly so, or if it is, then densely hairy or powdery on undersurface . . .   go to #16

15 a. Shiny green, holly-like, small leaf; common scrub oak of California—California Scrub Oak, *Quercus dumosa* . . .   turn to page 138

    b. Dull gray-green, holly-like, small leaf; common scrub oak of the southwest—Scrub Oak, *Quercus turbinella* . . .   turn to page 139

16 a. Dark green leaves on upper surface; powdery yellow or gray undersurface; golden-hairy when young; a large oak— Canyon Live Oak, *Quercus chrysolepis* . . .   turn to page 134

   b. Leaves dull green, blue-green or brownish-green . . .   go to #17

17 a. Convex, dull, green leaves; spiny to almost smooth; in California on serpentine areas— Leather Oak, *Quercus durata* . . .   turn to page 138

   b. Bluish-green or brownish-green leaves with almost right-angle notches on the undulate margin; pale and hairy underneath when young; corky cup—Wavy-leaf Oak, *Quercus undulata* . . .   turn to page 140

18 a. Leaves deeply lobed (at least ½ way to mid-rib) lobes end in bristles; lower leaf surface about same color as upper; scales of cup thin and papery—Black Oak, *Quercus kelloggii* . . .   turn to page 127

   b. Leaves with shallow or deep lobes; no bristle . . .   go to #19

19 a. Blue-green leaves; shallow lobes—Blue Oak, *Quercus douglasii* . . .   turn to page 131

   b. Leaves shiny or dull green, but not blue-green; conspicuously lobed . . .   go to #20

20 a. Deep green leaves; lightly hairy undersides; found in Wyoming and Colorado south into Arizona, New Mexico, and Texas—Gambel Oak, *Quercus gambelii* . . .   turn to page 130

   b. Dull green leaves 6-13 cm long, pale underneath; deeply furrowed gray bark; deep cups—Valley Oak, *Quercus lobata* . . . turn to page 128

   c. Shiny green large leaves (9-17 cm); pale green and somewhat hairy on underside; dark with shallow grooves, broad ridges; shallow acorn cups—Oregon or Garry Oak, *Quercus garryana* . . .   turn to page 129

BLACK OAK
(California Black Oak)
Quercus kelloggii

Black Oak is a big-growing beautiful tree with wide-spreading branches if it has the room. It is found mainly in oak grasslands, particularly north-facing slopes in lower altitudes, or valleys in mid-altitude. It is very different from most western oaks, resembling the Black Oaks of the east—especially because of its big, jagged leaves. It generally grows to be from 16-25 meters (50-75') tall and 35-60 cm in diameter, especially if in groves.

The trunk often bends or leans, and is clear of branches for 4-7 meters. Mature trunks are dark blackish-brown, deeply furrowed only near the base. The upper trunk and branches are quite smooth and are a grayish-brown. Year-old twigs are reddish.

As new leaves come out, they tend to be very reddish and very fuzzy. During the summer they are big, thin, bright, shiny deep green. This is an oak that colors in the fall to a clear yellow-orange—dramatic with its dark trunk and branches. The smooth leaves are very characteristic, for they are large (10-18 cm), deeply lobed, and each point is tipped with a tan bristle.

It blooms in April and May, with the acorns maturing the second season. They grow to be 2.5-3 cm long (1-1½''), with a short stem

and the cup wider than deep. The scales of the cup are thin, with a membranous margin, but become thickened near the stem.

The Black Oak is not as long-lived as the Valley Oak, probably maturing in 175 years. The wood is fine-grained but porous. It grows from Oregon to San Diego in both the Coast Ranges and Sierra Nevada of California. In the Coast Ranges it is mainly east of the crest or on the cooler slopes. In the Sierra Nevada it is found between 1,000 and 7,000 feet, particularly in the Yellow Pine areas.

VALLEY OAK
(Roble, California White)
Quercus lobata

The scientific name describes the leaves of this beautiful oak, for they are lobed, not toothed or spiny. The upper surface is dull green, the lower is paler and yellow-veined. Valley Oak is a good common name, for it usually grows in open valleys with deep soil. It never grows in groups—always scattered individuals. It's a big oak, the largest of all American oaks, probably living for 300 years, and characteristically has a short thick trunk producing pendulous, arching, large branches.

The thick gray bark is deeply furrowed, and, as someone said, looks as though some huge cat scratched it all the way down. The large branches also have this characteristic bark. There are occasional cross furrows, often diagonal, but the main pattern is the

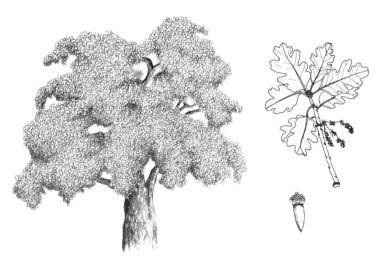

long deep furrow. It may grow to be 20-30 meters high and as wide at the crown, with the trunk diameter up to 4 meters.

Valley Oak blooms in March and April, the male catkins and the tiny female flowers appearing as the new leaves unfold. The long (3-5 cm) acorn is a rich brown, beautifully tapering from its deep cup to the tip; the upper row of scales of the cup are tiny, the lower ones are thicker and warty. The acorns mature in just one year. In a good year, a tree will produce hundreds of acorns, which are definitely sweetish, and are edible. The acorn, though it germinates easily when covered by fresh litter, doesn't germinate well when it just falls on thick grass.

The leaves may vary, even on the same tree, from 4-10 cm long (1½-4"). They usually do not color in the fall—only turning tan or brownish before they drop off. The margin is smooth, but deeply lobed from 6-10 times.

Valley Oak grows in the valleys and low grassy hill areas of California from Mendocino County south to the Los Angeles area, on the eastern slopes of the Coast Ranges, interior valleys, and western foothills of the Sierra Nevada—always where soil is deep. In rolling foothill areas, you tend to find the Valley Oak in the bottoms, merging with Blue Oaks as you go up the hills. It is usually nowadays only found as an old tree, often with huge broken branches.

OREGON OAK
(Garry's Oak, Post Oak, White Oak)
Quercus garryana

A large oak usually 17-20 meters tall, but may be several meters taller, 45-75 cm in diameter (18-30"), with a short trunk producing big branches that reach upward (not arching as *Quercus lobata*). The lower ones may extend horizontally.

The bark is fairly thin, with shallow grooves and broad ridges, with grayish scales. The leaf buds are covered with rust-colored hairs and the young twigs are very hairy. The shiny, smooth, deep green leaves are irregularly round-lobed. They are thick, big, 9-17 cm (3.5-6.5"), tough, and are pale green and hairy underneath.

The Oregon Oak produces its blossoms in April to June, the acorns maturing in one year. The cup is shallow, the acorn plump (3 cm long) and sweetish. The scales of the cup are thickened towards the base.

Flourishes in valleys and slopes from Vancouver Island south through western Washington and Oregon to the central Coast

Ranges of California, from sea level to 3,000 feet. It grows largest in deep humus soils of Washington and Oregon. It may be much smaller in drier, more gravelly soils.

GAMBEL OAK
(Rocky Mountain White Oak)
Quercus gambelii

This is the very common deciduous oak of the whole Rocky Mountain area, from southwestern Wyoming south, in foothills and on canyon walls, throughout Utah and western Colorado, into western Nevada, in most of Arizona except the most southwestern part, most of New Mexico except along parts of the southern and eastern border, and into western Texas and Mexico.

The firm leaf is deeply lobed (more than half the way to the mid-rib), the lobes are rounded and have no prickle. The leaves tend to vary in size—from 5 to 15 cm (2-6''). The leaf resembles the California White Oak, with its deep, rounded lobes, but the Gambel Oak leaf is thicker and the underside is lightly hairy. The upper surface is a soft, very dark green, the under surface only slightly paler.

The gray-brown bark is fairly thin, but rough and scaly, the twigs stout.

The broad, round acorns are up to 2 cm wide (¾''), the small, thick-scaled cup covering one half of the nut. They mature in one year, and are sweet (and fattening), good for eating.

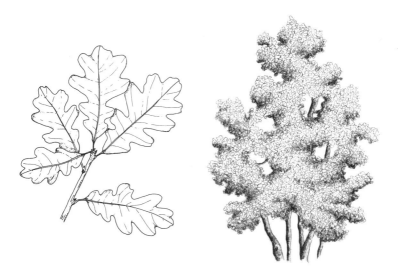

Gambel Oak tends to grow in clumps as tall shrubs or trees to 10 meters (30'), usually many-trunked or growing as a thicket. It spreads by underground runners. However, big, separate, individual trees may grow to be as tall as 17 meters (50'). It is the common deciduous oak throughout the Rocky Mountains, coloring whole slopes red in the fall.

BLUE OAK
Quercus douglasii

An oak easily recognized by its thickish blue-green leaves. It can be spotted from a distance because of its color, which is very similar to the Digger Pines with which it grows in the Sierra foothills and in the higher areas of the California Coast Ranges. The leaves are usually irregularly lobed or they may be almost smooth-margined.

The tree is quite easily recognized by its silhouette—most easily, of course, when its leaves are gone—for then the pattern of its many branches, which divide again and again into smaller branches in a very regular pattern and all end in a beautifully rounded crown, the network resembling the blood vessels in a kidney. At first the branches are big and fat, but soon become smaller. The twigs are very brittle, and you often can guess it's a Blue Oak by the litter under it.

The bark is gray, thinnish, and checkered, and is easily flaked off—very different from the deeply furrowed Valley Oak. These

can be easily distinguished where they intermingle. The Blue Oak also tends to be a medium-sized tree 10-18 meters (30-50') tall, with short, stout branches quickly dividing into smaller branches. In good locations, however, the Blue Oak can become fairly large.

The blue-green leaves, somewhat hairy, are variable in outline—from almost smooth to irregularly lobed and toothed. The Blue Oak is one of the last to loose its leaves in the autumn, and also one of the last to leaf out in the spring.

The acorns are usually small (2-4 cm) in shallow warty cups, but vary from being slender to quite plump.

Blue Oaks grow on wooded, rolling hills and drier slopes; in the low Coast Ranges it borders chaparral areas, but is found with Digger Pine in the higher areas, and especially found with Digger Pines in the Sierran foothills. It grows from north-central California to southern California with White Oak and Live Oak.

INTERIOR LIVE OAK
(Sierra Live Oak)
Quercus wislizenii

Interior Live Oak is a medium to large-sized tree 8-25 meters (25-75') tall, with thick branches which generally form a very round crown. In excellent locations it may grow much larger (there are tremendous ones on Mt. Diablo in central California), but in dry areas, it may even by shrub-like. In many ways it can be confused with the Coast Live Oak, *(Q. agrifolia)*, especially as a young tree, since they do grow side by side in many areas. Generally, the Interior Live Oak never grows as big or develops as large branches as

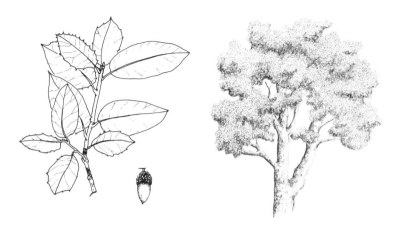

does the Coast Live Oak. The evergreen leaves are 2.5-3.5 cm (1-1½'') long, stiff and *flat*, not with edges curled as *Q. agrifolia*, and much thicker. The margin may vary from smooth to spiny; the leaves on mature trees usually will not show much margin variation, and tend to be smooth. However, young trees, and even new shoots on mature trees, will have leaves that are toothed and spiny right beside ones that are smooth. The upper surface is dark green, the undersurface is shiny yellow-green. They usually stay on the tree for 2 seasons, falling the second summer.

Bark is light gray except on the larger branches or trunk where it will be darker, fissured, and somewhat scaly, but not loose.

The Interior Live Oak blooms from March to May, the acorn maturing the second year, as is typical with the Black Oak group. The acorn is long (2.5-3.5 cm), slender and pointed, much narrower at the base where it is held by the deep cup with long thin reddish scales.

It is a common oak on interior slopes, woodlands, rolling hills and chaparral from Mt. Shasta through the Coast Ranges, the central valley of California, and the Sierran foothills to northern Baja California, mostly below 5,000 feet.

COAST LIVE OAK
(California Live Oak, Encina)
Quercus agrifolia

This is the Live Oak of California found in the hills and valleys of the Coast Ranges, extending from the north into Baja Califor-

nia, usually below 3,000 feet. It is often found growing with Valley Oak *(Q. lobata)*, Blue Oak *(Q. douglasii)*, and Buckeye *(A. californica)*.

The bark is generally gray and smooth, with irregular fissures on big branches or the trunk. It was used in the past, along with bark from the Tanbark Oak, for tanning leather. The tree usually is 10-25 meters, with a short stout trunk and great spreading branches forming a broad dense crown.

The shiny dark green leaves are 2.5-7.5 cm (1-3'') long, stiff, leathery and usually convex on the upper surface: the edges tending to roll under. The margins are usually spiny, the undersurface of the leaf green, and it is hairy at the junction of mid-vein and side veins.

The Coast Live Oak blooms from February to April with the tiny female flowers in the axils of the leaves in the new twig growth, the male flowers scattered among the leaves from buds on last year's growth. The acorns take only one year to mature, and are held in a thin-scaled turban-like cup which is very fuzzy inside and fairly shallow. The nut is slender and pointed, 2.5-3.5 cm long.

CANYON LIVE OAK
(Gold-cup Oak, Maul Oak, Iron Oak)
Quercus chrysolepis

The Canyon Live Oak is a beautiful evergreen oak which has many forms—in size, shape, manner of growth and leaf shape. In good locations it makes a fabulous tree 20 meters tall, but in dry ex-

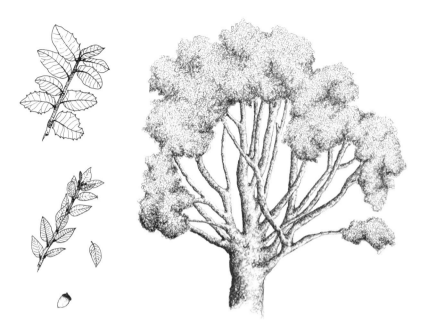

posed areas it may be almost shrub-like. Typically it produces many big branches, unless in crowded areas.

The leaves are so varied that at first the tree may be hard to recognize. The leaf margin may be smooth or variously toothed. Young leaves on new growth tend to be more spiny than those on older twigs, but variations may occur even on just one small branch. The leaves are stiff, leathery, and somewhat blue-green above. When young, they are powdery yellow-green below, but grayish-powdery as they mature.

The bark is ashy-gray and smooth and has rectangular scales which are not loose. The twigs are very woolly-hairy when young, turning dark red-brown as they mature and often keeping the hairiness.

It blooms from April to June, the acorns varying almost as much as the leaves in shape and size! They usually are thickish, 2.5-3 cm long in thick yellowish cups, and take 2 years to mature. The cup is shallow with thick walls and very fuzzy with rusty or yellowish wool (hence one of the common names).

Canyon Live Oak grows in open woods, canyons, moist slopes and flats below 6,500 feet from southern Oregon to Baja California; also in the mountains of Arizona, New Mexico and into Mexico.

EMORY OAK
(Black Jack Oak, Encino, Desert Live Oak)
Quercus emoryi

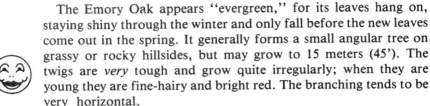

The Emory Oak appears "evergreen," for its leaves hang on, staying shiny through the winter and only fall before the new leaves come out in the spring. It generally forms a small angular tree on grassy or rocky hillsides, but may grow to 15 meters (45'). The twigs are *very* tough and grow quite irregularly; when they are young they are fine-hairy and bright red. The branching tends to be very horizontal.

The leaves are medium size (3.5-5.5 cm), however, in a dry location, they can be quite small (see picture). They are leathery and rigid, shiny, somewhat yellow-green above, and paler, but still shiny, on the undersurface. They may be irregularly spine-tipped or smooth-margined—on the same tree—and tend to be very flat. There are two fuzzy spots of hairs at the base of the blade on the underside.

The acorn becomes almost black when ripe; it is small but very edible, even without roasting. It was a staple food of the Indians and of course is eagerly eaten by birds and small mammals. The thin cup is thickly woolly inside and holds about ½ of the nut. The soft, hairy scales are papery thin. The wood is very dark and heavy.

It is generally found about 4,000 to 6,000 feet elevation, but may go as low as 3,000 or up to 7,000 feet.

The Emory Oak is the main evergreen oak of the southwest, found in canyons, hills, mountainsides, and higher range lands, but at lower elevations than the deciduous Gambel Oak.

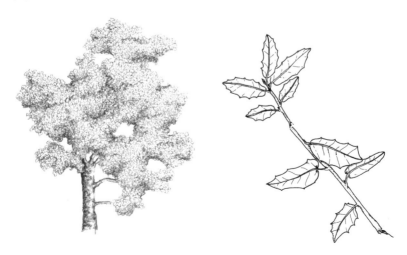

ARIZONA WHITE OAK
(Encino Blanco)
Quercus arizonica

This is the biggest oak of the desert southwest, growing to be 20 meters tall (60') in moist canyons. The lower branches are big, heavy, and almost horizontal.

The young twigs are very woolly, later turning smooth and quite dark. The ashy bark is fissured, with broad ridges of long thick scaly plates.

The firm, leathery leaves vary in size from 2-8 cm (1-4"). They are dull deep blue-green on the upper surface, the under surface covered with tan-colored thick, fine down. The mid-rib is yellow and noticeably wide, especially as seen on the lower surface. The leaves are not truly "evergreen," for though they last over the winter, they fall in the spring.

The dark, red-brown, shiny acorn is 1.5-2.5 cm long, about one-half of it set in the cup. The cup scales are reddish and hairy, quite thickened from about the middle to the base. The acorns are very bitter.

Arizona White Oak grows in the Live Oak areas of central and southern Arizona, southern New Mexico, south into Mexico in the high range lands, canyons, and mountain sides, but below the elevation where Yellow Pine and Gambel Oak grow.

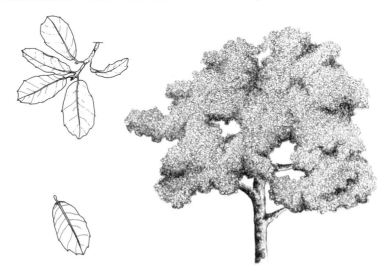

LEATHER OAK
Quercus durata

Leather Oak is shrub-like which may become tree-like (up to 5 meters), and frequently looks like a natural bonzai. It often grows in clumps, and is found mostly in chaparral areas of California. It's a stiff oak, with hairy twigs and small (1.5-2.5 cm), evergreen, leathery, dull green leaves which are convex on upper surface and have short spines or teeth (or variable to almost smooth margin).

The bark is light grayish brown and somewhat scaly. The thick, warty cup encloses about half of the squat acorn, abruptly pointed at the tip.

The Leather Oak grows mainly on serpentine areas in chaparral hills and mountain slopes of Coast Ranges from northern California to the south-central region and in the middle regions of the Sierra Nevada.

CALIFORNIA SCRUB OAK
Quercus dumosa

Although this is usually a scrub oak, it may grow to be 2-4 meters tall, often growing in groups. The branches are short, stiff, and angled.

The bark is thin, grayish and scaly. The leaves and acorns are exceedingly variable, even on the same plant. The "evergreen" leaves are dark and shiny, but do not last for 3-4 years as most evergreen oaks—they fall as the new leaves come out. In the springtime, as the new leaves are unfolding, the color of this oak may be yellow-green from the color of the new leaves and the yellowish male catkins. The leaves are small, 1.5-2.5 cm (½-1"). They are usually irregularly spiny, but may be smooth and typically have one deeper lobe about mid-way in the margin on each side. They tend to be flat, not convex.

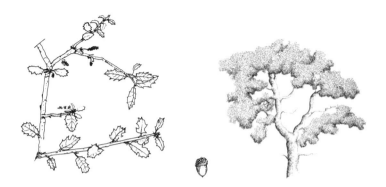

The California Scrub Oak blooms from April to June; the acorn is broad at the base and usually rounded at the tip. The cup is deep, holding about ½ of the acorn. The scales are united and warty near the bottom.

It is a common oak in the chaparral areas, in foothills and mesas, but not in serpentine rocks. It grows from the northern Coast Ranges and western slopes of the central part of the Sierra Nevada of California, south to Baja California.

SHRUB LIVE OAK
Quercus turbinella

This is *the* common Scrub Oak of the pinon-juniper areas of the southwest—very widespread in Arizona and into southwestern New Mexico. It is also found in southern Colorado, Utah, southern Nevada, southeastern California, Baja California and western Texas. It is very similar to the Scrub Oak found further north, *Q. dumosa*. It generally is just a shrubby tree from 1-4 meters tall (3-12').

The leaves are dull gray or gray-green, the margins toothed, each tooth with a short spine. They are almost like a gray holly leaf, 1.2-3.5 cm long (.5-1.5"). The mid-vein is very noticeable on the lower surface. The young twigs are thickly covered with a grayish-yellow wool.

The small yellow-brown acorns usually have a short stem, are fairly round, and come abruptly to the tip. The cups are about as deep as wide—about 1 cm. This oak hybridizes with other Scrub oaks, particularly *Q. grisea*.

ENGELMANN OAK
(Mesa Oak)
Quercus engelmannii

This is a smallish oak 5-18 meters tall (15-55') with a rounded crown, somewhat resembling the Blue Oak *(Q. douglasii)* in silhouette and leaf color. However, this oak is only found from southern California into Baja California. The bark looks somewhat like that of Valley Oak *(Q. lobata)* with deeply furrowed, wide- ridged, cross- checked pale gray-brown bark, but this oak has thin scales on the surface. The twigs at first are reddish-brown and thickly coated with short hairs, later becoming smooth.

The trunk is short, usually 50-75 cm in diameter (20-30''), with many stout horizontal branches. The mature leaves are very distinctive, for they are thick, deep blue-green or gray-green but variable in size, shape, and margin. They may be any size from 3 to 8 cm in length and the margin may be almost smooth, just barely irregular and wavy, lobed, or definitely toothed. The leaves are "evergreen," but they do not stay on the tree for 3-4 years as do most live oaks but stay on only during one winter.

The dark brown, streaked, blunt acorn is 2-2.5 cm long (¾-1''), the downy deep cup enclosing almost half of the nut. The scales at the base of the cup are thickened by a vertical ridge.

This is the dominant oak, often growing with Coast Live Oak *(Q. agrifolia)*, on the dry rolling hills and low mesas of southern California below 4,000 feet.

WAVY-LEAF OAK
Quercus undulata

The leaves with wavy edges and curled-under margin give the common name to this interesting oak of the southwest. It is found in the piñion-juniper woods, usually as dense thickets. Generally it is shrub-like, but may be a small tree in moist areas.

The firm leaves are 2.5-5 cm long (1-2''), somewhat oblong in shape, with shallow, almost right angle notches, wavy margins, and each notch or tooth with a small spine. The leaves are pale bluish-green or brownish-green, shiny above, pale brownish beneath, and hairy when young.

The brown, barrel-shaped acorn is small, 1-1.5 cm (½''), and the corky cup covers one third of the nut.

Wavy-leaf Oak is commonly found with piñons and junipers from southern Nevada, Utah, and Colorado, throughout most of Arizona and New Mexico (except southwestern-most Arizona or southeastern New Mexico) and into Texas.

NET-LEAF OAK
Quercus reticulata

The most characteristic feature of this scrub oak is the very noticeable heavy network of raised veins, especially seen on the undersurface.

The leaf is concave on the upper surface and is very gray, thick, and leathery, with a barely irregular margin. Sometimes there are a few teeth, though usually there are none, especially on leaves on lower twigs. The leaf tends to be quite oblong in shape.

However, the acorns really distinguish this oak, for they are small, usually in 2's and 3's and stand on a *long* stalk—a very un-usual feature.

The Net-leaf Oak is found in Texas, New Mexico, central to southeastern Arizona and into Mexico. Nowhere is it abundant, but is often found in canyon areas and the plateaus in quite large clumps. Excellent examples can be found around Prescott, Arizona. It tends to be a tall shrub or small tree.

GRAY OAK
(Scrub Oak)
Quercus grisea

This oak is a small, round-topped low tree or shrub of the desert hillsides of the southwest, usually from 6-15 meters (18-45'), but can be taller in moist areas, especially when not in windy situations. It is usually found in groups or thickets, with the taller trees in the middle, the outer ones shrub-like.

The branches are yellow and hairy—a definite characteristic, for they are this way for several years. The dusty gray, evergreen leaves are oval, nearly smooth-margined, with branched white hairs underneath and a somewhat hairy upper surface where it can be rubbed off easily, and then the leaf shows dull-shiny. They are usually about 3 cm long (1.25"), leathery but thin. Most of them are heart-shaped at the base.

The small, slender acorns are usually paired, 1-2 cm long (½-¾"), and are on a 1 cm hairy stalk. The cup is shallow, enclosing about one third of the nut.

Gray Oak grows in the pinon-juniper areas in the middle and upper elevations of the mountains from southeastern Arizona to New Mexico and Texas (where it is particularly common), and into Mexico, often found with Emory Oak.

There are other oaks of the arid southwest, many of them scrub-like and usually found only in limited areas:

Silver-leaf Oak, Mexican Oak *(Q. hypoleucoides)* is found in the mountains of southeastern Arizona, southwestern New Mexico, the Big Bend area of Texas and northern Mexico. It usually grows in shrub-like clumps with almost black, deeply furrowed bark. The leaves are thick, leathery, evergreen, long, and slender with smooth margins except a tooth or two near the tip. The undersurface has thick woolly hairs, making it noticeably silver. The upper surface is

shiny dark green with the margin rolled under. It has a small acorn with a thick shell, the cup thickly woolly inside and silvery at the base outside. Silver-leaf Oak may grow as a spreading-crowned tree in moist canyons, along with cottonwoods and sycamores, at elevations of 5,000 to 7,000 feet.

Mexican Blue Oak, *(Q. oblongifolia)* grows in the dry foothills and mountains of central and southern Arizona, especially south of Tucson, into Mexico and southeastern New Mexico. It is abundant at Carlsbad Caverns. The evergreen, grayish or blue-green leaves are 2.5-5 cm long with smooth margins and is oblong in shape, as its scientific name implies. In winter the leaves are rusty-bronze, and fall before the new leaves come out. The bark is ashy-gray with almost square, platy scales. The acorns are dull light brown, small, and the cup has red-tipped coarse hairs. This oak is usually tree-like, but tends to grow wider than tall.

DOUGLAS HACKBERRY
Celtis douglasii

Douglas Hackberry grows in widely scattered localities in Washington and Oregon east of the Cascades, in southeastern Idaho, the Wasatch Mountains of Utah, the eastern foothills of the Rockies in Colorado, the Grand Canyon region, and southern Arizona.

The leaves are 5 cm long (2''), heart-shaped at the base, but unevenly so, and coarsely toothed. The upper surface is sandpapery and the netted veins become very noticeable in the late summer.

The flowers are inconspicuous but develop into small, shiny, orange-brown, edible berries which hang, often in pairs.

Douglas Hackberry always seems to grow naturally in fairly dry localities.

NETLEAF HACKBERRY
(Palo Blanco)
Celtis reticulata

Netleaf Hackberry gets its common (and scientific) name from the very noticeable network of veins in the leaves. It grows as a small, scraggly, slender-trunked tree to 10 meters (30').

It grows in grasslands, along the dry washes and river valleys of the southern parts of the southwest. It is often parasitized by both insects and mistletoe.

The ashy gray bark on the crooked spindly trunks is rough and ridged. The young shoots are often long and arching. The dark green leaves are 2.5-6 cm long (1-2.5"), unevenly heart-shaped at the base, with wavy but smooth margins, tapering gradually to a slender tip. They vary considerably in both size and shape. The leaf is definitely sandpapery to the touch, rougher in one direction than the other, and veins have scattered long hairs.

The small shiny yellow or orange-red fruits are 1-seeded, sweet, and edible—totally unlike the fruit of the elm trees, though hackberries belong to the same family. The fruits are .5-1 cm long (¼-½").

It is sometimes called Palo Blanco in the southwest, perhaps because of its very whitish wood. It is common along the Colorado River, into central and southeastern Arizona and through New Mexico, and south widely into Mexico and Texas.

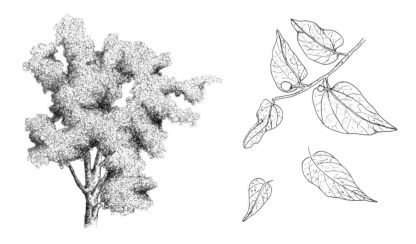

CALIFORNIA BAY
(California Laurel, Oregon Myrtle)
Umbellularia californica

California Bay is a common, easily recognized tree of southern Oregon and California. It grows in both the Coast Ranges and Sierra in higher foothill or low mountain areas, canyons, and damp slopes where there is constant moisture. It is an evergreen tree with very aromatic leaves and bark. Once it is smelled, it is never forgotten. The dark green leaves may be 7-15 cm long (3-6'') and 1.5-4 cm wide (½-1½'') though healthy trees tend to have very uniform-sized leaves 11-12 cm long. They are smooth edged and very regular in shape, though may have a flattened or even tiny notched tip. They continue producing new leaves all summer as the twigs grow, so the trees tend to have very dense foliage.

The tree may be 15-30 meters or taller, producing a dense crown of closely-leafed branches; many trees branch in such a way and are so thick you can scarcely see the trunk except close to the ground. The trunk itself is usually many-branched, the branches often large. In less damp areas, they may form tall shrub-like clumps, but in choice locations they will become huge trees more than a meter in diameter with large straight trunks and big branches.

The young bark is smooth and gray-brown; the mature bark is thin, dark, red-brown and scaly. The 3 cm fruit looks like a

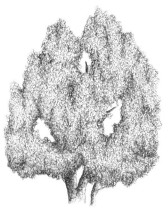

yellow-green plump olive. It has a leathery covering around a thin-shelled light-colored seed. The small yellowish flowers are produced in spring in clusters at twig ends. They have no petals, but have 6 yellow-green sepals, 9 stamens with very noticeable orange glands at their base. Bees are very active around the blooming trees. The fruits mature in the fall and are carried off and tucked away in all sorts of "hiding places" by the blue jays. When they fall naturally, they are carried by water and individual trees may spring up far from the parent tree.

The Laurel family has many trees and shrubs which are spicy or aromatic besides having commercially useful wood. Cinnamon, camphor and avocado all belong to this family. The bay leaves sold as a spice are from the Grecian Laurel *(Laurus nobilis)*. California Bay leaves can also be used as a seasoning though it is stronger-flavored and some people seem to be allergic to its odor.

CALIFORNIA SYCAMORE
(Buttonball, Buttonwood, Plane Tree)
Platanus racemosa

Sycamores are beautiful, picturesque, easily distinguished trees with their chalky white or pale green, smooth bark. Even old trees show this characteristic bark on the large branches and upper trunks, though the bark at the base becomes thick, ridged and gray-brown. The bark on young trunks and all branches doesn't thicken as the tree grows, but peels off in platelets and patches as new bark is produced underneath. The newly exposed bark is olive green but it gradually changes color through gray and tan to chalky white.

There are three species in the United States, all very similar and all moisture-lovers, found along stream banks or in damp valley habitats. The eastern species *(P. occidentalis)*, is usually larger than its western relatives and is widespread from Maine to Nebraska and south to Florida and Texas. The southwestern sycamore *(P. wrightii)* extends into Mexico, while the western species *(P. racemosa)* is found from central California south into Baja California. It is common along streambeds of the interior valley and below 4,000 feet elevation in the western Sierra foothills and in the Coast Ranges.

The tree usually has many large branches and may even branch near the ground in a V or J shape. Or a big side branch may extend horizontally with others extending at all sorts of curves or angles;

even the main trunk often leans. The smaller branches develop a very zigzag growth pattern.

The California Sycamore usually grows 45-75 cm (18-30'') in diameter and 12-20 meters (40-60') tall, but enormous old giants 28 meters high and 150 cm in diameter are found.

The palmately lobed leaves are thick and big (12-28 cm; 5-11'') and as wide as long. There is much variation in the lobing—usually there are 5 lobes, sometimes with deep notches between the middle and two upper side lobes (see illustration). The lower notches may be quite reduced. The leaves are densely but minutely hairy, especially on the midveins and undersides. The hairs fall off after a bit and some people are allergic to this "hair" as it floats in the breezes. The new twig growth is also hairy with a golden fuzz. The upper leaf surface is light yellow-green; the lower surface is quite pale and shows especially when the wind is tossing the branches. The wood, even when living, is extremely brittle and large branches may break off very unexpectedly.

The flowers are tiny but grouped into round balls or heads. In the spring, as leaves begin to unfold, the male flowers are produced, hanging on slender stems from last year's growth. They are greenish-yellow and pea-sized. The female flowers are clustered into brown marble-sized balls with bristles standing out all over, each group hanging on threads from the tip of new growth. These

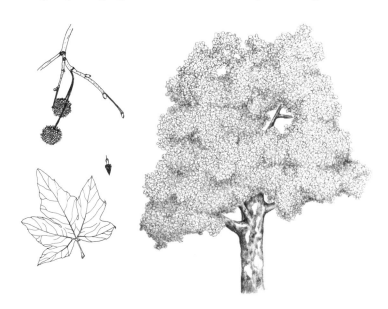

are the very noticeable "buttonballs." Because of these flower-heads, the tree is very interesting in the early spring as the tiny young leaves are unfolding. The male heads soon wither, but the female heads gradually grow and ripen into rough spheres 2-3 cm in diameter (1''). The mature seed balls ripen by early winter, the balls break, and bristly seeds are released, each in a tuft of fuzzy hairs.

The Southwest Sycamore *(P. wrightii)* for a while was considered just a variety of the California species for its only difference seems to be the leaf shape and fruit stem. The leaf lobes are much longer and more slender and have peculiar frequent little blips on the margin, and the fruit heads have a noticeably longer stalk. It is the largest tree of the desert (up to 26 meters). In Sycamore Canyon in the Coconino National Forest, there is a giant, 5.5 meters around! It is abundant wherever there is regular running water, and flourishes in altitudes from 2,000 to 7,000 feet.

CURLLEAF MOUNTAIN MAHOGAHY   S. W. SYCAMORE

CURLLEAF MOUNTAIN MAHOGANY
Cercocarpus ledifolius

The Curlleaf Mountain Mahogany is a picturesque, crooked, much-branched tree, usually 5-7 meters tall (15-20'), but may be taller, or an irregularly branched twisted shrub.

The grayish leaves are narrow and long (1-3 cm) with the margins rolled under—this is the distinguishing characteristic of this mahogany. They are thick and leathery with many tiny hairs on the undersurface. They stay on the tree for two or more years.

Mountain Mahogany is noticeable because of its twisted shape, but particularly so when the fuzzy long-tailed achenes cover the tree, making it appear frosted or silvered, glistening in the sun.

It is found in arid mountain regions on poor gravelly soils, though it will stand richer soils (and there grows bigger). It grows from eastern Washington to Montana, Wyoming, and Colorado; from eastern Oregon, in the Basin Ranges of Nevada and Wasatch of Utah, south to New Mexico and on the eastern slopes of the Sierra Nevada in California, frequently with Piñon Pine.

CALIFORNIA MOUNTAIN MAHOGANY
(Birch-leaf Mountain Mahogany)
Cercocarpus betuloides

The California Mountain Mahogany grows from 3-8 meters tall (9-25'), has small dark green leaves, somewhat narrow at the base, but widening to the middle where the margin becomes notched, gradually curving to the rounded tip—the notching or teeth becoming smaller towards the tip. The parallel side veins are very noticeable, especially on the undersurface, running to the tip of each tooth. The leaves tend to look somewhat like a tiny birch leaf. The bark is scaly, but this flakes off, leaving smooth, gray, hard bark which is somewhat "sandpapery."

It blooms in April or earlier, the seeds developing long (6-10 cm) hairy tails. The reddish wood is very hard and fine-grained.

It is a common small tree or shrub in the chaparral areas from southern Oregon to Baja California and into Arizona where it is more often called the Birch-leaf Mountain Mahogany.

TOYON BERRY
(California Holly, Christmas Berry)
Heteromeles (photina) arbutifolia

This tall shrub or small tree (2-10 meters) rarely has just one trunk— often there are many of more or less the same size, with

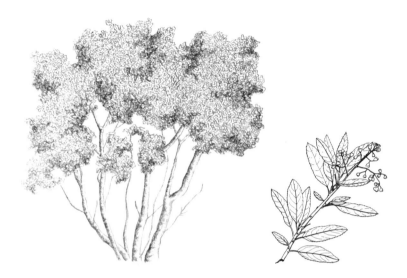

new slender shoots regularly growing from the base.

It blooms from June to July with clusters of white or creamy flowers which develop into red berries.

This is a common shrub-tree in the cooler chaparral area, oak woodlands and canyons below 4,000 feet from Baja California in the California Coast Ranges to the Mt. Shasta area, and in the western foothills of the Sierra Nevada.

The leaves are pointed at the end, have short-toothed margins and vary from 5-10 cm long (2-4''). They are dark green above, yellow-green below, and somewhat pungent. The bark is gray-brown and somewhat sandpapery to the touch.

SERVICE BERRY
Amelanchier alnifolia

Service Berry (more often pronounced "Sarvice" Berry) is really just a shrub—frequently long and lanky, but because of its height, may be considered tree-like. It may form thickets from one to two meters (3-6') high or at times a slender tree to 10 meters (30').

The leaves are one of the most characteristic features, for they are quite wide for their length and are smooth-margined except near the tip, where they are sharply toothed. They are rather grayish-green, often with a tinge of red—especially along the leaf edge.

The flowers are pure white, and petals quite long and turned every which way, giving the flower a "shaggy" appearance. They are in loose clusters, the ovary developing into an urn-shaped purplish-black fruit with the remnants of the sepals at the top.

It is found abundantly in hilly or low mountain areas from 100–6,000 feet near the coast from Alaska to California, in the Sierra, and the mountains of southern California. In the Rockies it is found mainly between 5,000 and 8,000 feet, and also found east through the northern states (Idaho, Montana, etc.) and Canada.

WESTERN BLACK HAW
Cratageus douglasii

Black Haw is a shrub or small crooked-branched tree to 10 meters, often forming thickets. The most noticeable feature is the presence of stout, sharp thorns in the leaf exils. The twigs are reddish, the trunk reddish-brown with a few shallow fissures. Mature leaves are 2.5-8 cm (1-4") long, leathery, often glossy deep green above, with sharp shallow teeth above the smooth-margined base. Some leaves have a shallow lobe or two.

The many-branched, fuzzy, flowering stem is at the twig end, each flower at the tip of a short peduncle. The sepals are long, curved, and pointed, with some glands along the edges. There are 5 white petals and many stamens. The dark purple or black shiny edible fruit is 1 cm long with persistent sepals. It ripens in the fall and falls soon thereafter. It grows between 2,500 and 4,000 feet on flats in mountainous areas from British Columbia south to the mid-Sierra Nevada of California and east through Idaho and Montana.

PRUNUS

A group of small trees or tall shrubs, usually deciduous, producing a fruit with a pit or stone (as a cherry) which is called a "drupe." The clusters of whitish, 5-petaled flowers appear before or with the leaves. Many of them are useful for jams and jellies; some are bitter.

HOLLY-LEAF CHERRY
(Islay, Evergreen Cherry)
Prunus ilicifolia

Holly-leaf Cherry is well-named, for its thick, spiny, glossy, green leaves resemble those of holly. It may be a shrub or a small tree 2-8 meters high (6-25'). Either form is many-branched and with thick evergreen foliage forming a rounded crown. The twigs are smooth and reddish or yellowish. By the time a large trunk is developed, the color has changed to dark red-brown, furrowed and cut into squares.

The leathery leaves are regularly spine-tipped, 2.5-5 cm long (1-2") and many of the leaves seem to be partly folded up along its main vein. The undersurface of the leaf is much lighter in color.

The flowers are thickly clustered in fairly narrow spikes 3-6 cm long (1-2½"), each flower about 1 cm across with 5 cream colored petals and many stamens.

The fruit is a deep red or red-purple drupe, the pulp thin and tart, but edible. The pit is large, smooth, thin-shelled, and veined.

It generally grows on open hills, slopes or in ravines, preferring

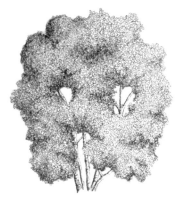

moist sandy soil but often growing on drier slopes in the chaparral from San Francisco Bay, south, in the Coast Ranges of California to Baja California below 5,000 feet.

CHOKE CHERRY
Prunus virginiana var. *demissa*
Prunus meganocarpa
Prunus virens

Choke Cherry may be just a shrub or grow to a small-sized tree, 7 meters tall (21'), but it always is erect and stiff-appearing.

The bark is gray-brown with shallow irregular ridges, the young branches smooth and reddish, and the twigs hairy, with a definite acrid odor if crushed.

The soft, green, leathery leaves are finely toothed, particularly from the middle to the tip. The leaf is 3-8 cm long (1-3''), broader at the base, and tapers quickly to the tip. There usually are a pair of glands at the base of mature leaves. The undersurface is pale and somewhat hairy.

There are many short, leafy side branches. Near the tip some of these develop flowering spikes 5-10 cm long (2-4'') with several tiny white, 5-petaled flowers. They bloom in May and June. The fruit is a small drupe which is not quite 1 cm. It is round, dark red or deep purple when ripe, and has a large cherry-like pit. It is bitter to eat when raw, especially if not fully ripe, but makes a good deep red jelly. It tends to jell very solidly and has a fairly strong flavor; a mixture of apple juice and Choke Cherry makes a better jelly.

It often grows abundantly, and is especially noticeable along trails and roads on brushy mountain slopes, canyons, flats, and stream borders, 1,500–7,000 feet elevation. It is found south

through Washington and Oregon (where it is abundant) to California in both the Coast Ranges and the Sierra Nevada, and east to Idaho.

Prunus meganocarpa, the Black Choke Cherry, is the species found especially in the Rocky Mountains and the Great Basin area, south to New Mexico and west to British Columbia, Washington, Oregon, and the eastern slope of the Sierra Nevada. It is very similar to *P. demissa* but has many more flowers crowded into its flower spike, the leaf is bright green, the twigs are smooth, and there are no glands at the base of the leaf blade. The drupe becomes almost black when ripe and is extensively gathered for jelly.

The Southwest Choke Cherry, *(P. virens)*, has somewhat pointed, glossy, black cherries, its leaves shiny green above, pale beneath, and is almost evergreen. It may grow as tall as 12 meters along streams. It is found in the mountainous areas of northern Mexico, western Texas, southern New Mexico to central Arizona from 5,000–8,000 feet.

BITTER CHERRY
Prunus emarginata

Bitter Cherry may be a good-sized tree from 10-14 meters (30-42'), a small tree of 6 meters (18'), or a shrub, with thin, shiny, red bark with scattered white spots on the young twigs. The branches and smaller trunks are silvery—especially so in the winter and spring; the main trunk is smooth, dark reddish brown, and re-

sembles the Orchard Cherry. The young twigs, leaves, and fruit are very bitter and acrid-smelling if crushed or broken.

The leaves may vary in thickness and size (3-5 cm), with shrubby forms tending to have smaller, thicker ones. The margin has tiny, glandular, rounded teeth.

Clusters of small cream-colored flowers, like tiny cherry blossoms, are produced near the branch tips, blooming as the leaves are expanding—in April and May near the coast, in June and July in higher elevations. They are fragrant if you haven't masked the odor by crushing a leaf or stem. The fruit is a very small, bright red, very bitter drupe with a pointed pit.

This is a very adaptable tree, growing abundantly from sea level on Vancouver Island to 5,000 feet, and even as high as 9,000 feet in the mountains in the southern part of its range. Found along streams and on mountain slopes from Vancouver Island and southern British Columbia east to Idaho and Montana, south through Washington and Oregon to southern California. Also found in western Nevada and the San Francisco Mountains of northern Arizona.

SIERRA PLUM
(Klamath Plum)
Prunus subcordata

The Sierra Plum is a stiff deciduous shrub or small tree with crooked branches and short thorn-like branchlets. It usually grows on dry rocky slopes, often with chaparral, but can grow on moister slopes.

The twigs are red and shiny, the older bark browner and smooth. The leaves are oval to roundish.

The Sierra Plum grows from Oregon, south, in both the Coast Ranges and Sierra Nevada below 6,000 feet, to south central California. There are several varieties, all producing different colored drupes—from yellow to bright red to dark red, 1.5-2 cm long.

WILD RED PLUM
Prunus americana

The Wild Red Plum is found from central New Mexico, north through middle elevations in the Rockies in Colorado, Utah, Wyoming, and eastern Montana, and extensively in the east. It mainly grows on warm slopes or cleared areas, along streams, fences or ditch lines.

It is quickly recognized as a plum by the many white flowers blooming before the leaves bud out, and in the late summer by the small bright red plums with tiny dots on the skin. The skin of the edible fruit is thick and tough but the inside is juicy and yellowish.

The leaves are 5-10 cm long (2-4''), and have regular, small-toothed edges and a wrinkled surface with wavy margins. This plum tends to grow as a slender-trunked tree, or may even be shrub-like, with somewhat drooping branches. It spreads not only by its seed but also by root sprouts, often forming thickets.

MOUNTAIN ASH
(Sitka Mountain Ash, Rowan)
Sorbus sitchensis

Mountain Ash is a beautiful small tree or shrub, especially when its large flat-topped cluster of small white flowers have matured into bright orange-red berries. The warm-tan smooth bark has characteristic ring-like leaf scars on its surface.

The pinnately compound leaves are 14-17 cm long and arranged alternately on the branch. (Elderberries have somewhat similar leaves, but they are opposite.) The leaflets are sessile except the one at the tip. There are nine to thirteen leaflets which are serrate nearly to the base—if they are toothed only near the tip, it is the Western Mountain Ash *(Sorbus occidentalis)*, which usually is only a shrub.

The stems often are quite reddish and are hairy at the leaflet base; the veins on the underside are also fuzzy.

Mountain Ash blossoms in late May and June, the berries ripening by fall.

Mountain Ash grows in canyons, along streambanks, and on moist mountain slopes to 9,000 feet, often forming impenetrable jungles with their many trunks and long, down-curving branches. They are found from Alaska south through British Columbia, in the Cascades of Washington and Oregon and the northern Coast Ranges of California and the Sierra Nevada to Yosemite, then east throughout the Rocky Mountains.

TREES OF THE PEA FAMILY

Amazingly enough, a good proportion of the desert trees belong to the pea family. The leaves are alternate, often with stipules (though commonly the stipules are reduced to spines). Most of them also have thorns along their branches, some have branchlets that end in spines, many of them very sharp or hooked. Most of them have pinnately compound leaves, often double-pinnately compound.

The flowers are often in clusters of tight spikes with many long stamens. The fruit is usually a legume (a flat two-sided pod that opens on one edge), but it may be a spongy pod that doesn't open till it disintegrates.

CATCLAW
(Una-de-gato)
Acacia greggii

Catclaw is a stiffly sprawling, irregularly branched shrub or small tree that you won't want to get too near. There are stout *curved* spines on the dark gray branches—practically impossible to take hold of any piece without getting scratched or hooked. The

spines are like hooks, and are on all the twigs and branches. The dead branches are even worse to grab hold of, for the spines are very sharp—beware when looking for camp cooking wood.

The leaves are small (2-5 cm overall), and double-pinnately compound. First you'll notice the 2 to 3 pairs of pinnae (first division leaflets), arranged alternately on an angled leafstalk. Then each pinna has 4-6 pairs of small pinnules .2-.8 cm long. The leaf appears very fine and "soft" because of the many tiny pinnules, but take care, for these "soft" leaves will not keep the spines from scratching you.

The tiny yellow flowers with many stamens are in dense spikes 2-5 cm long (¾-2"). They are in clusters near the branch ends and bloom from April to June. This is an excellent honey tree. The seed pods are 2-12 cm long (¾-5"), twisted and ribbon like, narrower between the seeds. The seeds are dark brown.

Catclaw is common in gravelly washes, hillsides, and canyons below 6,000 feet in the deserts of southern California, east through Arizona and New Mexico to Texas and into Mexico and Baja California.

BLUE PALO VERDE
(Border Palo Verde)
Cercidium floridum

The Blue Palo Verde is a twiggy tree up to 7 meters tall, with slender spines at the leaf axils and slender branchlets. It is seldom seen with leaves, for they usually appear in March and then soon fall. Even when the leaves are on the tree, they aren't very noticeable, for there aren't many of them and they are in tiny pairs.

The leaves are small, the short leafstalk has one pair of pinna, each with 2-3 pairs of small pinnules oppositely arranged (so there is no end leaflet). They are most often closed on each other. There is a small spine just above the leaf base.

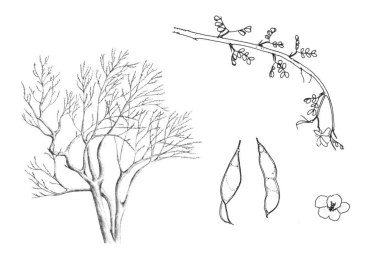

The trunk is short and is gray-green or blue-green except near the base, where it is brown or reddish-brown with thick platy scales.

The crinkly yellow flowers are about 2 cm across, growing singly or in small clusters, and bloom profusely from March to May. The upper petal is broader and different in shape from the others—it has a claw and is marked. This tree is excellent source of honey. The flat seed pods are 5-10 cm long (2-4''), with several seeds, the ripe pod often very constricted between the seeds. Both ends of the pod are very similar in shape and size.

This desert tree is found in sandy areas, but particularly along washes below 3,000 feet in southern Arizona, southern deserts of California and to Baja and northern Mexico.

This tree tends to look bluish, and is sometimes hard to tell from Yellow Palo Verde at a distance if there are no leaves. Blue Palo Verde has spines at the leaf base; Yellow Palo Verde only has spines at twig tip. Both Palo Verde seem to have thousands of little branchlets—probably because their branches do most of the food-making for the tree.

YELLOW PALO VERDE
(Foothills Palo Verde, Little-leaf Palo Verde)
Cercidium microphyllum

The Yellow Palo Verde has smooth, light yellow-green bark, especially on the branches and twigs. The bark of mature trees may be gray and irregularly ridged, but only near the base. The trees

may be anywhere from two to eight meters tall. The branchlets are spine-tipped, other than those, there are no spines. The two pinnae arise directly from the twig (no leafstalk). The leaves come out in opposite pairs lower on the stem; single pairs near the tip. Each pinna then divides into 4-8 pairs of pinnules that are very tiny, the whole leaf only about 2.5 cm long. The end pair of pinnules is usually larger than the lower pair.

The flowers are pale yellow, the upper petal whitish or greenish, and bloom from April to May, usually later than the Blue Palo Verde. It may hybridize with that species and it is a good honey plant. The flattened pod is 4-8 cm long with one to four seeds, constricted between the seeds and ending in a long beak.

This Palo Verde can live in drier areas than the Blue Palo Verde, so it is more likely the desert tree of mesas and hill areas of southern California deserts, to the south and west part of Arizona, into Mexico and Baja California up to 3,000 feet elevation.

HORSE-BEAN
(Mexican Palo Verde, Jerusalem Thorn, Retama)
Parkinsonia aculeata

Horse-bean is a shrub or low-growing roundish tree to 10 meters (30'). It is closely related to the genus *Cercidium* in which the trees are commonly called "Palo Verde." This tree also is bare of leaves most of the time.

In this genus there are 3 spines at each leaf node—a pair on each side and then a longer one that is actually part of the leaf base, the

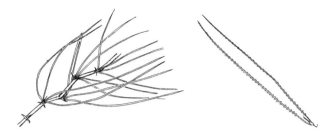

two pairs of rachis arising directly from it. Just above this triple spine (i.e., at the leaf node) there are 4 long (30-40 cm—12-15'') drooping flattened "streamers." These are really the two pair of leaf "stems"—the rachis. If the tree has leaves, they will be tiny and look as though the rachis has minute scallops along the edge. Actually there are just 2 pinnae, each compound, with 4-25 pairs of tiny pinnules. The round green twig zigs at each node.

The bright yellow flowers turn red as they age; the upper petal, has red spots and is the largest, the stamens are shorter than the petals. The flowers are usually in fairly long spikes. The seed pods are swollen around each seed, constricted between them.

This is often found naturalized now from Arizona to Florida, in the West Indies, Mexico to South America, and is often planted in desert areas, for it is very resistant to dryness and alkali. In places where it gets adequate water there are flowers on this small tree most of the time. It is found growing naturally in Mexico, southwestern Arizona, and the Rio Grande Valley of southern Texas.

DESERT SMOKE TREE
(Indigo Bush)
Dalea spinosa (psorothamnus)

A beautiful smoke gray "ghost" is the way you'll generally see this small tree or large shrub, appropriately called the Desert

Smoke Tree. When it blooms, and you see its incredibly blue, pea-shaped flowers you'll understand why it received its other common name—Indigo Bush.

Smoke Trees may be up to 8 meters tall (25'), very crooked and angular, with complex branching, and are ash-gray in color. The many twigs are stiff and spine-tipped, they and the branches gray and velvety when young, the lower and older branches rough and peeling, the trunk gray-brown and scaly, with deep furrows. The leaves are small and scattered, only lasting for a few weeks after the rains.

The bright blue-purple flowers are in spikes 2-3 cm long (1''), on a slender hairy stem, blooming from late May to July. A thin 1-seeded pod is produced.

Common in the washes of southern California deserts and Baja California, east to Arizona and New Mexico.

DESERT IRONWOOD
(Mexican Ironwood)
Olneya tesota

Desert Ironwood is a many-spined shrub or tree up to 8 meters tall (25'), the branches spreading widely. The twigs are very hairy the first year, then smooth, pale greenish, and by the third season are tan with many sharp spines .3-.6 cm long (¼''). The thorns are slender and short, but very sharp.

It is an evergreen tree, though the leaves only live one year. They are on the tree till the flowers wither, then are pushed off by the next crop of leaves, so the tree is never really bare of leaves. Iron-

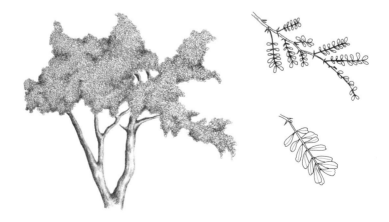

wood trees seem unusually "dense" as compared to most desert trees since, though the leaves are small, there are many of them. The leaves are gray, pinnately compound, from 3-19 cm long—the size of both the leaflet and length of entire compound leaf will vary greatly with amount of moisture (see illustration). As with many of these desert members of the pea family, the leaflets are in pairs, so there is no tip or end leaflet. There are 3-8 pairs of tiny leaflets, often with a tiny notch, and the end leaflets are usually the largest. A *pair* of spines is located below each leaf.

The common name is well-earned, for it has such dense, heavy wood that a chunk of it dropped in water will keep dropping—it is too heavy to float.

It is abundant between the town of Desert Center and the Colorado River and in the areas north of Phoenix. It is found along the washes and in the desert valleys of southeastern California, Arizona, into Mexico and Baja California below 2,000 feet.

HONEY MESQUITE
(Algaroba)
Prosopis juliflora

Mesquites usually have several trunks or one short trunk with many very crooked branches. The branches are bent and twisted, but often in an angular arch.

There are pairs of spines above the leaf axils and the double-pinnately compound leaves are very characteristic. There are one to two pairs of pinnae from just below the spines on a fairly long leafstalk. Then each of the pinna has 7-17 pairs (14-34 separate ones) of small pinnules. The leaves are very light green, particularly when they first unfold, but later turn gray-green. Because of being double-pinnately compound, they appear "fern-like."

The tiny, fragrant, greenish flowers have long stamens and grow in tightly packed slender spikes (appearing much like long slender catkins), blooming first in April and then often again in June.

One to several long, flat, straight, or slightly curved seed pods develop from each flower cluster. There is spongy tissue between the seeds, so they appear bumpy as the seeds mature. The pods do not open as do most members of this family; the seeds are only released as the pod disintegrates. The pods are 10-15 cm long (4-6") and about 1 cm wide, each holding 10-20 seeds. They are sweet.

There are two common varieties: *P. velutina*, with leaves, twigs, and pods which are all velvety and have fine hairs and *P. torreyana* which has no hairs.

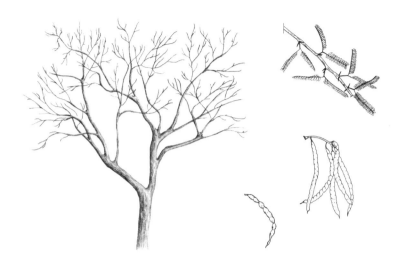

Honey Mesquite commonly grows along desert washes and the river gravels of southern California, southern Nevada and Utah, and then east through Arizona and New Mexico to Texas and through Central America to Venezuela. It has recently spread amazingly and uncontrollably over many areas.

SCREW-BEAN MESQUITE
(Tornillo)
Prosopis pubescens odorata

Screw-bean is a many-trunked tree that grows to 10 meters (30'). The branches are usually very crooked and angled. The twigs are pale and slender. There are paired, stout, whitish spines each 1 cm long, just above the leaf axis.

The leaves, 2-6 cm long, are double-pinnately compound with the rachis forked to form two paired pinnae, each with 3-7 pairs of pinnules less than 1 cm long. The leaf is soft-feathery appearing.

The tiny yellow flowers are crowded into narrow spikes 4-7 cm long (1.5-3'') with very long stamens extending beyond the petals. They bloom intermittently over a long period of time. Many pods develop from each spike and are very unique and recognizable because they are tightly and spirally coiled like a stout spring 2.5-5 cm long. The pods are sweet eaten raw.

The wood is hard but not very strong. It grows on desert washes and canyon areas below 2,500 feet elevation from the California deserts eastward to southern Utah, Arizona, New Mexico and into Texas.

WESTERN REDBUD
(Judas Tree)
Cercis occidentalis

Redbud is a small deciduous tree or tall shrub with almost round or kidney-shaped leaves which are heart-shaped at the base. It is generally low-branched or even many-trunked and forms a dense round clump, a spot of light green in the hills. The abundant, bright pinkish-purple, pea-like flowers bloom before, or as, the new leaves unfold.

The bark is grayish and thin with short vertical marks and spots, and new growth very dark purple-brown.

The pale green leaves are glossy on both sides and round or kidney-shaped, with the base often heart-shaped, the four side veins all branch from the mid-vein at or about the same place.

The flowers appear in clusters before, or just as, the new leaves are unfolding, produced on last year's growth. Often the large empty pods of the previous year's crop will still be hanging on their thin stems. They are 4-7 cm long, dull red-purple and hold several flat seeds.

Redbud grows in dry or rather dry rocky soils—foothill slopes and borders of streams from northern California, south in both the Coast Ranges and the Sierra Nevada (where it is more abundant) to San Diego County, east to Utah and western Texas.

CRUCIFIXION THORN
Canotia holacantha

There are at least three different plants, belonging to three different genera, which have the common name of Crucifixion Thorn; however this is the one that is found most often.

It is a shaggy-looking grayish-green mass of stiff, upright, round twigs from grayish, fissured branches and shaggy trunk. Each twig is round, fairly long, and has many sharp-tipped round spines that are 4-8 cm long (1.74-3.5''). These all contain chlorophyll and are capable of making food for the plant which otherwise has no leaves. All the twigs, spines, and most of the branchlets point upwards more or less vertically (the thorns at about a 35-45° angle from the stem). If the thorns grow at almost a right angle to twig, it is *Koeberlinia spinosa*, for that is its distinguishing charactertistic.

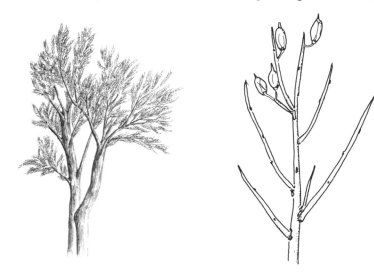

All this stiff upright growth gives the plant a vertically brushed or broom-like appearance.

The fruit is a persistent capsule, in ones or twos on twig tips near the top of tree. It is oval, has a sharp point at the tip and is 1.5 cm long (½"). The sharp tip is at first reddish and the capsule green, but eventually all turns blackish.

The tree may become 20 feet tall and is scattered throughout much of central Arizona—especially in areas northwest and southeast of Phoenix; also found in eastern California. It is a peculiarly unattractive "tree-mass."

FREMONTIA
(Flannel Bush)
Fremontodendron californicum

The buds and new twigs have this similar "sand-grainy" hairiness. Last year's and older twigs are a rich red-brown and usually not sand-grainy. This texture gives it the common name of "flannel bush" though it is far from soft.

There are many tough, flexible branches, often from near the base, so Fremontia appears many-trunked and develops a large, open, spreading shade. These branches usually develop many fairly long side branches, with the leaves and flowers on short side branchlets.

The dark seeds are produced in a bristly, angular, persistent capsule 2.5-3.5 cm in diameter.

Fremontia is found on gravelly slopes, especially on granitic soils from 1,500–5,500 feet elevation in chaparral, Yellow Pine and

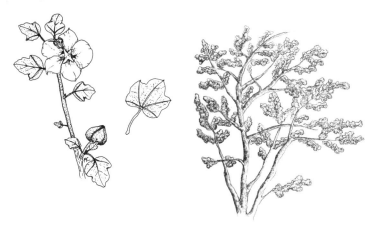

Piñon Pine areas. Occasionally it is found in the California Coast Range, but more abundantly in the western Sierra Nevada from the Mt. Shasta areas, south to San Diego and east into Arizona. In some areas, it has been extensively planted along freeways, for it does not require much water—in fact, overwatering will kill it.

This small tree or large shrub (up to 6 meters) is most noticeable when in bloom (April-June), for then it is covered with many bright yellow, rather large (3.5-6 cm in diameter) wide-open flowers. The persistent withering flowers turn burnt orange and gradually fade to tan. The 3-lobed short-stemmed dark green leaves are 2-5 cm long. They are thick and "sand-grainy" on both sides (i.e.—rough and granular-hairy), but especially underneath. They are evergreen.

DESERT WILLOW
(Desert Catalpa, Mimbre)
Chilopsis linearis

Desert Willow gets one common name from its very long, narrow, willow-like leaves, but when it is in flower, it never would be mistaken for a willow. Another common name, Desert Catalpa, is more appropriate, for it truly is related to the Catalpa tree, as shown by the large whitish, pinkish, or purplish 2-lipped tubular flowers. They have a bright yellow spot in the throat.

The leaves are only 1 cm wide (⅓") and usually about 15 cm (6") long, but they may be as long as 25 cm (10"). They often are sticky when young, becoming smooth and darker green as they mature.

The seed pods are also long (7-20 cm; 4-8") and slender (.75 cm). They mature in the early fall, but stay on the twigs most of the

winter, gradually splitting in two to release many light, flat, fringe-winged seeds which are easily carried by the wind.

It is generally a very thin, "weeping" tree, even when growing in good locations, for the leaves and pods all are thin, long, and drooping, the branchlets long and flexible.

Desert Willow may be a large but sparse shrub or small tree, and is widely distributed in southern New Mexico, most of Arizona (except the northeast), southern Utah and Nevada, southeastern California, and well into Mexico. It is mainly found along or in dry washes and river areas and commonly lines roads.

MAPLES

Key to Species of Maples (Acer)

1 a.   Leaf simple, with 3-7 or more serrate or toothed lobes . . .   go to #2

    b.   Leaf pinnately compound with 3-5 leaflets, serrate or toothed . . .   go to #4

2 a.   7 or more shallow lobes, serrate, leaf usually less than 10 cm wide—Vine Maple, *Acer circinatum* . . .   turn to page 170

    b.   3-5 deep lobes, serrate or toothed; mature leaf usually 10 cm or more across . . .   go to #3

3 a.   Large leaf, often 20 cm across, very deeply lobed, long petiole—Big-leaf Maple, *Acer macrophyllum* . . .   turn to page 172

    b.   Smaller leaf with broad blunt lobed and rounded teeth; southern Rockies and desert mountains—Big-toothed Maple, *Acer grandidentatum* . . .   turn to page 172

    c.   Smaller leaf with 3 large lobes, a lobe much smaller at either side; more or less sharply toothed; leaves may vary in size and configuration—Rocky Mountain Maple, *Acer glabrum* . . .   turn to page 171

4 a. Leaf pinnately compound with 3 thin serrate leaflets; samaras only on female trees—Box Elder, *Acer negundo* . . . turn to page 173

b. Leaves pinnately compound with 3 or 5 leaflets and simple palmately veined 3-5 lobed leaves—Rocky Mountain Maple, *Acer glabrum* . . . turn to page 171

VINE MAPLE
Acer circinatum

The Vine Maple can be an erect shrub or small tree to 10 meters (30'), but it often leans or can even be vein-like. In the northwest it definitely is a tree, and one of the most beautiful maples around Vancouver. The deciduous leaves are 7-12 cm wide, and as high— so the leaves are almost round except for their fairly shallow lobes. Usually there are 7-9 lobes, but there may be as few as five and as many as eleven.

The young leaves are hairy and reddish, but smooth when mature except for a tuft of hairs near the base. The trunks are smooth— gray with a tint of green overwash when young, just plain gray when mature with scattered short horizontal dashes; the base of larger trunks may have shallow cracks.

The 5-10 flowers are borne on a slender 2-leafed stem. They appear reddish, and most of the flowers are male. The flower cluster often sets just one fruit. The double samaras develop as the seeds mature, the two seeds themselves tail to tail, so the wings form a straight line—not angled as most maples. These begin turning red by early summer and are brilliantly crimson when ripe.

Vine Maple is found in moist woods, and on slopes and stream banks west of the Cascades from British Columbia to northern California below 5,000 feet elevation.

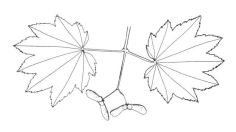

ROCKY MOUNTAIN MAPLE
(Dwarf Maple, Sierra Maple)
Acer glabrum

This mountain maple is generally a smallish tree from 2-6 meters (6-18') with many slender trunks and numerous opposite small branchlets. However, in moist locations, particularly in the northwest, it grows regularly to tree size and is one of the very abundant and noticeable maples there. It is most often found growing in clumps.

The shiny leaves are palmately lobed and veined, usually from 2.5-5 cm wide (1-2"), but they may be much larger in moist situations. Generally, there are three large lobes and two much smaller lobes.

Often the male and female flowers are on separate trees. The female flowers are generally clustered so they produce several samaras in a group, the wings at a 45° angle.

This maple can be found on semi-dry to moist slopes and canyon areas from 6,000 to 8,000 feet. It grows from southern California in the Sierra Nevada and in the northern Coast Ranges through Oregon, Washington and British Columbia to Alaska and east to the Rocky Mountains. It is also found further south at altitudes of 6,000 to 9,000 feet from South Dakota to New Mexico and Arizona.

BIG-TOOTH MAPLE
Acer grandidentatum

The Big-tooth Maple is a beautiful tree with deeply lobed, palmately-veined leaves somewhat similar to the Big-leaf Maple, but smaller leafed. It grows to be 18 meters tall (55') in favorable places, even in the southern, drier Rockies. The trunk tends to be short and stout.

The leaves are medium size, 4-14 cm, (2-5") with three to five broad, blunt lobes, the lobes again lobed or toothed.

The flowers often appear before the leaves, hanging in colorful catkins, the female flowers developing into rose-colored double samaras from the twig ends.

Quite common in the Rocky Mountains from southeastern Idaho, Utah, and southwestern Wyoming into Colorado, south to western Texas, and in the arid regions of the southern Rockies in

canyons and moist mountain soils of central and southern New Mexico, and most of the high mountain areas of Arizona except the northeastern and southwestern parts.

BIG-LEAF MAPLE
(Canyon, Oregon, White Maple)
Acer macrophyllum

This is usually a big tree, the biggest of the western maples, and well-named, for its palmately lobed leaves are enormous and often have stems almost as long as the leaf. The leaves may be 20-35 cm wide (8-14") with almost a satin-smooth finish. They are quite thick and become deep green, paler beneath, as they mature.

The bark is brownish or grayish, narrowly grooved or checkered. Because of its cool habitat, it is often patchy with interesting lichens. The bark on old trees is deeply furrowed with scaly ridges and usually brownish-red in color.

The samaras are large (each wing 6 cm long), with the seed portion thick and stiffly hairy. The 2 wings in this species never open

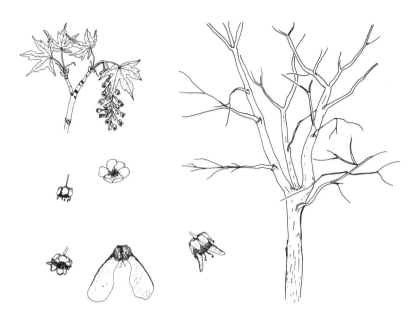

widely forming more of a U-shape. The tree usually produces vast quantities of samaras which may hang on the tree long after they mature in late autumn.

The Big-leaf Maple varies from a small tree 5 meters high (especially when in close groupings) to 30 meters tall as an individual, beautiful tree. The trunks tend to be straight and stout, 60-100 cm or larger in diameter (2-3'), and typically has several large branches. The twigs are dark red and shiny in the winter, brown and greenish and smooth during the balance of the year.

Big-leaf Maple is a common tree along streams and in canyons below 5,000 feet. It is found from Alaska, through British Columbia, Washington, Oregon (mainly west of the Cascades) and into southern California. It is found in both the Sierra and Coast Ranges of California, mainly on the cooler slopes. It is particularly abundant on the islands off British Columbia. It may grow as al-

BOX ELDER
(Ash-leafed Maple)
Acer negundo

This common tree grows over most of central and eastern North America; the Box Elders of the west are varieties, though the main species may be found as far west as parts of the northern Rockies. It is fast growing, usually with only a short gray-brown regularly furrowed trunk. Branching frequently occurs quite low on the trunk, and those branches often send up vertical shoots.

It grows 6-20 meters tall (18-60') and 30-90 cm (1-3') in diameter, and though probably it is a short-lived tree, old giants may be found along streambeds, where planted as windbreaks, or even as shade trees. It's not a desirable street tree or where ground litter is a bother, because it produces so many samaras and leaves.

The stems are smooth on all young growth, though they and the leaves are covered with fine, soft hairs in the western varieties—especially when young or on the underside of the leaf.

Though Box Elder belongs to the maple family, it has a very different leaf—it is compound—of 3 (or 5) leaflets; the eastern species may even have 7 leaflets which usually are not as thick as the thin-leafed western varieties. The end leaflet is always largest and each one is lobed or deeply toothed. The leaf itself has a long petiole.

The tree blooms in March and April, with the flowers appearing just before or as the new leaves unfold. The trees are either male or female (so you'll only have seeds from the female trees). The female flowers are in slender drooping racemes. The samaras are red when young, and become straw-colored when mature. They grow to be about 3 cm long. These may persist even into winter,

hanging in clusters from their thin stems. The male flowers hang in clusters on reddish or pink elongated, thread-like, fuzzy stems.

A variety, *Acer negundo* var. *californicum* has hairy twigs with thickish leaves. It is found below 6,000 feet in California from Shasta County to San Bernardino County, though rare in the Coast Ranges south of Santa Cruz. Another variety, *Acer negundo* var. *interius* is found south from Alberta along riverbanks, valleys and canyons of the Rockies to New Mexico and Arizona. It usually has only 3 thickish leaflets with softly hairy twigs.

BUCKEYE
(California Buckeye)
Aesculus californica

The Buckeye is one of the first trees to burst its big brown buds in the spring and the bright green leaves then unfold rapidly. It is also one of the very first to drop its leaves, even as early as mid-summer especially if it's a dry year or if the tree is in a drier location. The large hanging fruits are very noticeable.

The palmately compound leaves are large, 8-18 cm (3-7'') and ar-

ranged oppositely along the smooth grayish stems. There usually are five leaflets, but there may be seven, each leaflet finely toothed.

The tree grows 4-7 or more meters tall with picturesque branching. Often there are multiple trunks, so the trees are seen as clumps with broad round tops. They are seldom seen as isolated trees. The bark is smooth and very light gray.

The Buckeye produces lovely, long (15-20 cm), fragrant, many-flowered spikes at tips of the branches, coming into bloom usually in May. Most of the white or pale pink flowers are only males; a few near the tip have both male and female parts. The male flowers have 5-7 orange stamens. The fruit is large (2-4 cm diameter), round, glossy and brown. Usually only one or two fruits are produced per branch and hang on long stems. They are encased in a grayish, roughish, leathery, pear-shaped capsule.

It grows on damp hillsides, and in gullies and canyons. It is very noticeable, especially on the northern or cooler slopes in the California Coast Ranges and Sierra Nevada from Siskiyou County to Los Angeles County.

WESTERN SOAPBERRY
(Wild China-tree)
Sapindus drummondii

The Western Soapberry—often called Wild China-tree especially in New Mexico—is a tree of the southwest in the foothills and plains, and often planted as an ornamental. It may grow to be quite large with a thick trunk.

The pinnately compound leaf has 4-9 pairs of smooth-margined leaflets, the whole leaf being 12-20 cm long (5-8''). It is so arranged that the basal leaflets are more or less opposite each other, the leaflets getting more and more out of line toward the tip of the leaf. Though there is an even number, there is a leaflet at the apex.

The clusters of tiny white flowers bloom in May or June, and may be 15-24 cm long (6-9''). The fruiting stems tend to stand erect, so the clusters of translucent, yellow, ball-shaped berries are very noticeable. Each berry is about 1 cm in diameter (.5''), and is POISONOUS. Some people are allergic even to touching them and cattle do not eat them. The berry, however, can be used as a soap (hence the common name). Indians and Mexicans long ago found its soapy qualities, and chemicals from it can be used in varnish and floor wax. The leathery berry contains one to three dark seeds, each with a tuft of hairs.

Western Soapberry is found scattered in southern Colorado, central and southeastern Arizona, southern New Mexico, east into Texas and Louisiana, and south into Mexico.

CASCARA SAGRADA
(Bearberry, Bitter-bark, Wahoo)
Rhamnus purshiana

This smallish tree, or large shrub if there is not enough water, has a great variety of common names. As with others in this group, it has a bitter bark. If in favorable areas it will grow to 12 meters (36'), with a straight trunk and few branches. In other areas it will be shorter (6-10 meters), often multiple-trunked, but still with sparse branching. The branches are typically quite horizontal from the main trunks, and frequently are almost opposite.

The leaves are not really opposite each other but almost so. They vary in size if the tree has plenty of moisture and good soil. In the northern areas, the leaves are large and thin but in drier areas the leaves are smaller and quite hairy, especially on the veins. The upper surface is green and the veins are very indistinct, while the lower surface is yellow-green with very distinct hairy yellow veins. The

side veins are parallel to each other to the leaf margin, then curve abruptly. The leaf margin is finely toothed. There will be many leaves near the twig end.

The tiny 5-petaled flowers are in small umbels at the base of the leaves. One or two round black drupes about 1 cm in diameter develop in each umbel.

It is generally found below 5,000 feet on moist mountain slopes and canyons in mixed evergreen forests, with Yellow Pines and Redwoods from British Columbia south through Oregon and Washington in northern Coast Ranges and the Sierra Nevada foothills to the central part of California.

MOUNTAIN LILAC
(Ceanothus, Buckbrush, Tree Myrtle, Tick-Tree, Blue Blossom)
Ceanothus thyrsiflorus

This beautiful tall shrub or small tree has many common names—many of them referring to the lovely blue flowers that color whole patches in the spring. The flowers are tiny, but they are in clusters at the branchlet ends.

There are many different species of *Ceanothus*; most of them are shrubs, some are prostrate, but some become small trees. They hybridize freely in the wild, and because of their fabulous, fragrant, colorful blooms, have been selected and carefully hybridized by

nurserymen in California and Oregon where it is a favorite shrub or small tree in the gardens.

The trunk is tough and multiple or low-branched. The branches are slender, flexible, and trend upwards—or at least the tips of the sprays do. It has very twiggy growth, often at sharp angles to the main branch. The younger branches are greenish or bronze; young branchlets are grooved vertically. The base of mature trunks becomes quite gray and somewhat granular-appearing.

The leaves are 2-6 cm long, oval with a rounded or pointed tip and have three main veins from the base. They are dark shiny green above, pale beneath, the margin with tiny tan glandular teeth.

It is found abundantly on cooler slopes from southern Oregon to southern California in the Coast Ranges.

MOUNTAIN DOGWOOD
(Western Dogwood)
Cornus nuttallii

A slender tree from 3-20 meters tall with many branches tending to form flat sprays. The thin, heavily veined light green leaves are oppositely arranged. The branching also is opposite (especially noticeable at the growing tips).

The leaves may be as long as 12 cm, though more commonly 8-10 cm (3-4''). They color to lovely shades of scarlet, red and purplish in the autumn. When the leaves fall you can see the tiny squarish

flower buds for the next year, already formed, each at the tip of a twig. In the spring these start expanding, though the tips are seemingly "stuck together." Suddenly these will pop open and the white "petals" will increase in size rapidly and spread out flat—all of this happening before, or just as, the leaves start unfolding. It may bloom again in the fall, though not as heavily.

The blossom of this dogwood seems to have 4-6 large creamy white "petals" surrounding a button-like center. However, this center is made up of the many true flowers—a tightly packed group of tiny perfect flowers. The large whitish "petals" are really modified leaves called *bracts* enclosing the head of tiny flowers. The tiny flowers produce small, elongated berries which turn crimson in the autumn and usually stay on the tree after the leaves have fallen.

The bark is smooth, ashy-gray or brown, except on old trunks where it develops thin small scales. The twigs are green, turning to dark red—beautifully smooth and clean-looking.

This beautiful hardwood tree has a wide range in the Pacific states. It is found particularly on cooler slopes between 1,500 and 6,000 feet. It grows in mountainous wooded areas from British Columbia and Idaho south through Washington and Oregon to southern California in San Diego County, though it is not too common that far south. It is found in both the coastal mountains and on the western slope of the Sierra Nevada of California.

SILK-TASSEL TREE
(Quinine Bush)
Garrya elliptica

This small tree or bush is rather rare in the chaparral areas of Oregon and California, but it is so unusual that when seen, it is noticed. Now it is being used for freeway plantings, demanding little water or attention, but very attractive all year long. It is closely related to the dogwoods in many ways, but the flowers are so different it's put in a separate family—with only one genus found here in the west. The Silk-tassel Tree is known also as Quinine Bush because of the bitter bark, leaves, and fruit. It may grow 7 or 8 meters tall (21-24') in mixed chaparral or with Yellow Pine.

The evergreen leaves, 6-10 cm long (2.5-3.5") are very thick, with a smooth leathery upper surface. They are oppositely arranged. The underside is white-woolly, the leaf margins are somewhat irregular and the leaf tends to be wavy, and not lie flat. They somewhat resemble the leaves of the Coast Live Oak in form, but the

Silk-tassel Tree is fine-hairy on the undersurface of its leaves. The young twigs are densely woolly, becoming deep brown as they mature.

The flower is a hanging gray-green or yellowish "tassel" (hence the common name) at the branch tips, immediately attracting attention. The male and female flowers are borne on separate plants. The male flowers are usually 8-15 cm long (3-9") and covered with silky hairs. The female flowers are never as long, and tend to be compactly arranged and resemble a gray-green caterpillar with curly black hairs. These are the thread-like stigmas of each flower. The male flower hangs on for sometime, drying and then falling off; the female flower tassel enlarges into a thick-set multiple strand of berries which mature in the fall. Each berry has a thin covering over a bitter purplish pulp with one or two seeds.

MADRONE
(Madrona)
Arbutus menziesii

Madrone is one of the most beautiful broadleaf evergreen trees of the northwest. It grows as an arching, widely spreading tree from 13-40 meters tall (40-120'). Its distinctive bark, both smooth and colorful, and its big shiny green leaves make it particularly noticeable in the woods.

In the early summer the old layers of bark peel in thin flakes or strips, leaving the trunk a smooth pale green color that gradually changes to the polished rich red-brown color seen the rest of the

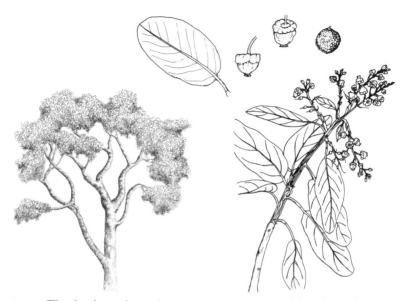

year. The bark peels each year except on the oldest branch bases
and lower part of the trunk, where it becomes grayish and narrowly
fissured.

The evergreen leaves are dark green, thick and leathery, pale on
the undersurface. The mid-vein is very conspicuous, the side veins
inconspicuous. The leaves are usually 7-14 cm long (3-5'') and 5-7
cm wide (2-3'').

Madrone blooms from March to May. The white or faintly pink
flowers are in many-branched clusters at the branch tips. The little
flowers are urn or lantern-shaped, with a narrow neck turned back
into 5 tiny lobes. The flower itself bulges regularly near the base,
usually in a pattern of 5. The tip of the green stigma can be seen as
you look down on the flower from the top. By late fall, the ovary
has developed into a bright orange-red, berry-like, mealy fruit with
a roughish or minutely warty surface.

It grows in cool locations in wooded areas and canyons, and on
slopes and flats; it grows best in rich soil, but will grow in rocky
soil, and often germinates best in new road cuts and disturbed soil.
It grows with Redwood, Tanbark Oak, Douglas Fir, and Yellow
Pine, and thrives best near the sea, for it likes the moisture of the
fog. It is most abundant and large-sized in the coastal belt of
southern British Columbia, through Washington and Oregon to
southern California; it is also found in the northern Sierra Nevada
to the Yosemite Park area, from sea level to 4,000 feet elevation.

MANZANITA
Arctostaphylos

There are many, many species of Manzanita in the west. Some forms are almost trees, while others are low prostrate shrubs. They resemble and are related to the Madrone—as is shown by both the flowers and the smooth red bark. Their simple leaves are evergreen, usually smooth-margined, and thick. They are mostly chaparral shrubs or almost-trees in the Coast Ranges and Sierran foothills. The trunk may be low-branched or there may be many trunks.

The whitish or pinkish lantern-shaped flowers hang in clusters, some species blooming as early as February. The various species seem to hybridize freely. The common name comes from the Spanish word meaning "little apple" referring to the small apple- like fruits which are edible, though they are not too tasty. The pulp is granular inside the thin dry skin and there are many seeds.

Many of the manzanitas develop a burl or enlarged root at the base. When a fire sweeps through an area, burning off the branches, sprouts will develop from this burl.

Arctostaphylos manzanita is one of the common species, found on dry slopes and canyon sides at elevations ranging from 300 to 4,000 feet from the northern interior Coast Ranges of California in the San Francisco Bay region north to Mt. Shasta and in the Sierra Nevada to the Yosemite area. It has bright green leaves, some forms are shiny, some dullish, 2.5-4 cm long (1-1.75"). It may grow to be as tall as 8 meters, with a broad crown, but usually only to 4 or 5 meters. The branches are crooked.

It blooms early—in February—with pale pinkish-white urn-shaped flowers. The "little apples" are a favorite food of many small mammals and birds. The bark is smooth, a lovely polished deep red-brown or even verging on purplish.

OREGON ASH
Fraxinus latifolia

Oregon Ash is often a good-sized tree to 25 meters (75') with a trunk often a meter (3') in diameter. In a forest there will be few side branches.

The gray-brown mature bark is thick, the wide ridges separated by regular, deep fissures. The pinnately compound leaf is large, 15-38 cm total length, with 5-7 smooth-margined leaflets. The end leaflet has a long narrow base and is usually bigger than the others. The side leaflets are sessile on the stem and may be 7-10 cm long. The veins are very hairy on the undersurface while the mid-rib is deeply grooved on the top surface.

The female tree produces samaras in small clusters, each samara on its own stem, many such clusters arranged oppositely on a long squarish stem. The samaras are long, narrow and separate.

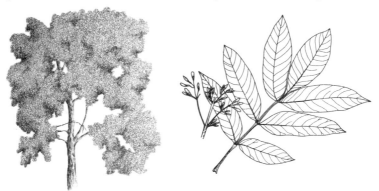

The large trees produce excellent, beautifully-grained wood, often used for plywood. It is tan in color with a silvery sheen.

Oregon Ash grows along streams and in valleys of the western mountains of Washington and Oregon and the Coast Ranges of California to the San Francisco Bay region, and to the central parts of the Sierra Nevada. It is found below 4,000 feet.

VELVET ASH
(Arizona Ash, Fresno Ash)
Fraxinus velutina

Velvet Ash is *the* common ash of the southwest. It is usually a medium-sized tree 8-12 meters (24-36') tall, but may grow to be 15 meters (45') and 30 cm (12'') in diameter.

The twigs are usually densely hairy, but this varies and they may be quite smooth. The bark is thin and soft, shallowly fissured and scaly, gray or reddish-tinged gray.

The thickish, opposite, compound leaves have 3-7 leaflets which are 10-15 cm (4-6") long. The margins tend to be regularly, but only shallowly, serrate from the middle to the tip. There is, however, much, much variation in the margin, the leaf thickness, size, and amount of hairiness. The angles between the leaf veins are almost always hairy on the underside. The leaves are smooth and pale green on the upper surface, pale and hairy on the undersurface; this hairiness gives it the common name of Velvet Ash.

The inconspicuous flowers appear before the tree leafs out, the large clusters of winged seeds maturing on the female tree by late summer. They are single samaras, each about 2.5 cm (1") long.

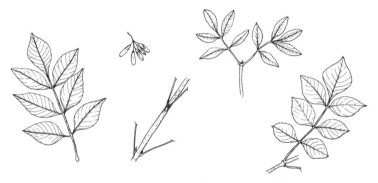

The Velvet Ash usually grows along canyon bottoms, streambanks, or water holes of the desert mountains up to 6,000 feet, often with cottonwoods. They produce quantities of seed. It is found in southeastern California, southernmost Nevada and Utah, from the northwestern to southeastern parts of Arizona, western New Mexico, the mountains of western Texas and into Mexico.

FRAGRANT ASH
Fraxinus cuspidata

The Fragrant Ash has compound leaves with 3-7 (9) small leaflets, each about 3 cm long (1.5"), pointed at each end. Only the tip leaflet has a stem—the others are attached right on the main rib. It may be a small tree, but often is quite shrub-like in dry areas. The flowers, unlike other ashes, have petals—and they are fragrant.

It is found in the western mountains of New Mexico and in the Grand Canyon areas.

SINGLE-LEAF ASH
Fraxinus anomala

The Single-leaf Ash is distinctive, as its common name suggests, in often having only a simple leaf, which is oppositely arranged. Ash trees typically have only compound leaves. However, this tree usually doesn't have just simple leaves. Leaves nearer branch tip usually have three leaflets (sometimes only 1), while those *at* the tip may have 5 leaflets (see illustration). In each case, the end leaflet, or the simple, single leaf, is almost round, 2.5-5 cm across (1-2''). All the leaflets are finely serrate, especially above the middle.

The leaves are oppositely arranged and leathery; it is particularly noticeable in that they dry leathery, not stiff and hard. The base of the leaf (or leaflet) is often quite unequal in shape.

The twigs are 4-sided, a distinguishing feature of this ash. In Arizona this ash is usually shrub-like or a small tree; in Utah and Colorado it is typically a tree.

The flowers (female and male are on separate trees) are inconspicuous and bloom before the trees leaf out. The fruit is a single samara 1-2.5 cm long (.5-1''), appearing in clusters.

Found near streams in sandstone areas particularly, from northeastern Arizona west to the Grand Canyon area, north into Utah and western Colorado.

ELDERBERRY
Sambucus (glauca) caerulea

Elderberry can be a shrub, a small tree or even grow as tall as 14 meters. It is usually 5-7 meters tall (15-20') with a straight, slender trunk 10-20 cm (4-8'') or larger in diameter, or may produce a group of trunks. The gray bark is somewhat yellowish or reddish, with a network of rough ridges. The leaves form a dense, usually round crown. The lower branches often droop and largish upright branches may develop from these, or from branches that have broken, so there will be sharp crooks in the bigger branch systems.

This season's growth stems are smooth, shiny and reddish with noticeable horseshoe-shaped pairs of leaf scars if the leaves have fallen. The leaves are compound, usually with 5-9 leaflets (sometimes 3) with each leaflet definitely but not deeply toothed.

The many tiny flowers are whitish, at branch ends, in a compound cluster, blooming from June through the summer. The fruit is a small grayish-appearing blue berry, but if you rub the "bloom" off, you'll see that the berry is blue-black when ripe. They develop in the somewhat flat-topped clusters, often very abundantly.

The Elderberry enjoys moist areas—valleys, slopes, ravines in rich but porous soil up to 10,000 feet; it becomes shrubby in higher altitudes. It grows with oaks, sycamores, Yellow Pine, Madrone, Big-leaf Maple (north) and White Alder (south). It extends south from southern British Columbia and Alberta to the Mexican border of California, eastward to Blue Mountains of Oregon, to northern Idaho and Wasatch Mountains of Utah.

Mexican Elder, *(Sambucus mexicana)* is a very similar elderberry, but with almost black berries because there is no whitish "bloom." Usually there are only 5 leaflets, which are thicker than *Sambucus caerulea*, and are hairy underneath. The Mexican species grows as a small tree 5-8 meters (15-25') with a swollen base. It is found from western Texas through southwestern New Mexico and Arizona to southern California, into Mexico and Central America.

COAST RED ELDERBERRY
Sambucus callicarpa

The Coast Red Elderberry is a smallish tree 2-6 meters high (6-18'), with a much-branched slender, smooth, woody trunk.

The dark green pinnately compound leaf has 5-7 leaflets, the margins have small but sharp teeth. It varies from 5-16 cm long, the veins with stiff hairs, especially on the underside which is also much lighter in color. These leaves are oppositely arranged up the greenish-purple side branches, ending in the purplish-stemmed flowering spray.

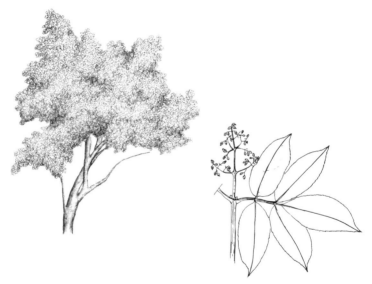

The small whitish flowers, in either flat or pyramidal clusters, bloom from March to June, producing small (.4-.5 cm) bright scarlet berries.

TEXAS MULBERRY
Morus microphylla

The Texas Mulberry grows as a small tree to 7 meters (21'), usually in a fairly round shape. It tends to resemble a small-leafed hackberry, and often grows with it. The leaf is similar to the cultivated mulberry in shape and variation (but much smaller). The margin will often have a "thumb-lobe," or a lobe on each side, or many of the leaves will not be lobed at all. It tends to be a fairly

small leaf, usually only about 4 or 5 cm (1.5-2''). The upper surface is very dark green and sand-grainy rough, the undersurface is paler with broad, hairy yellow mid-veins.

The flowers on male trees are in short spikes with red-tipped sepals and bright yellow stamens; flowers on the female trees have thick, rounded sepals. The edible berries are small, red to black, juicy and sweet. Birds and mammals eat them, and the Indians not only gathered the berries but actually cultivated the trees in some areas. The wood was used by the Papagos for their bows.

It grows in scattered groups, but is particularly found on limestone hills from central Texas westward to southern New Mexico and Arizona, north to the central plateau area of Arizona.

HOPTREE
Ptelea angustifolia

The Hoptree is a large shrub or small tree to 7 meters (21'), widespread in central and western New Mexico, central and eastern Arizona, southern Colorado and southern California. The twigs are dark purple or brown, the trunk slender.

The compound leaves have three bright green leaflets, almost as wide as long, and the bases of the leaflets are unequal. The underside is pale and densely soft-downy—a soft, thick-feeling leaf.

The greenish-white flowers are small and produce winged fruits. The papery wings have two light tan lobes, somewhat resembling hops—hence the common name.

Chapter VI

THE "INTRUDERS"

The trees in this short chapter are not natives, for they were brought here by people, either intentionally or by chance, from other places in recent times. But now these trees have "escaped" from their original plantings and have successfully established themselves either by seed, underground sprouts, or both, and now are so wide-spread along rivers or roads or waysides that they "seem" native. They have so successfully adapted themselves, they now are often competitors with the "natives."

Many of them, such as Eucalyptus and Pepper Tree, are planted along freeways, for not only are they picturesque but also can successfully tolerate the automobile pollution, and need a minimum of water.

EUCALYPTUS
(Blue Gum)
Eucalyptus globulus

The Eucalyptus is an aromatic exotic which has become so common in California that "natives" often feel that it is "native." It was brought to this country in the 1800s, particularly planted to produce wood for railroad ties. However, it was discovered that though it was tough and fairly long-lasting because of its oils, it warped badly and was very hard to do *anything* with unless it was cut and shaped while still green.

It is easily recognized from the characteristic peeling bark which separates into long strips, and finally falls or gets blown off, exposing beautifully smooth, warm-tan, whitish, or greenish wood underneath. The trunk may grow to be enormous, with tremendous side branches, often at picturesque angles. In fact, the Eucalyptus if grown far enough apart, becomes a beautiful tree. Even though they become very big, they have a shallow root system, and a combination of rainy weather and wind often brings many of them crashing down, or big branches will twist loose in a storm.

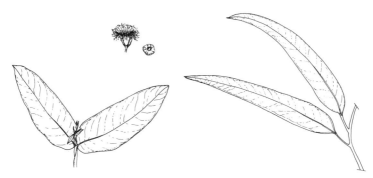

The leaves are leathery, long (18-25 cm; 7-10''), slightly curved and very aromatic. If the sun is hot, the area around a Eucalyptus tree is pungent with a camphor-like odor. The leaves have very prominent mid-ribs, which are especially seen on the lower surface, and very small indistinct side veins. The side veins are connected to each other by a vein running along the margin. The leaves hang vertically, with their edges oriented towards the sun rather than the flat of the leaf—necessary in the dry situations they thrive in.

Juvenile leaves are often different from the mature leaves. Generally, they are very blue-gray, much larger (both in length and width), are usually sessile, and oppositely arranged, rather than having a definite leaf stalk and an alternate arrangement as do mature leaves. The branchlet is 4-angled, twisting from leaf to leaf.

The flowers are showy with their abundant stamens popping up when the lid of the silvery-gray, woody bud is pushed off. Blue Gum has whitish stamens; many other species have bright red or orange stamens—making a very showy flower. The woody bud case becomes the seed capsule—in this species it is a flaring squarish-shape holding many small seeds. The trees bloom from May to July with hundreds and hundreds of flowers on one tree. Bees, hummingbirds and various insects feed on the nectar and pollen.

There are over 300 species of Eucalyptus, natives of Australia and Tasmania. They can usually be recognized, even though there are so many different species, by the aromatic leaves and the long strips of shreddy bark which expose smooth wood underneath. The leaves usually are long, narrow and pointed, but there is much variation.

Many of these trees are useful as ornamentals, for lumber, firewood, and several resins and gums. Eucalyptus oil is used for an inhalent. Many species have been planted here for these uses, and many have gone "wild."

PERUVIAN PEPPER TREE
Schinus molle

The Pepper Tree is a native of the tropical regions of South America, particularly Peru. Seedlings from cultivated trees are often abundant in the wild, having been scattered by birds. It is commonly planted, especially in southern California, and old, picturesque, big-limbed, gnarled-trunk specimens are abundant.

The evergreen, aromatic leaves are pinnately compound with 13-25 small leaflets, the whole leaf 20-30 cm long (8-12''). They hang from slender drooping or arching branchlets, producing a lovely lacy-patterned shade. The margin of the narrow leaflet is more or less smooth except near the tip where there will be 2-4 short teeth—sometimes there will be a few others along the margin.

The male and female flowers are on separate trees; they are small and whitish with five petals, blooming in June and July. The fruit is a rose-colored dry-skinned small drupe shaped like a small round, or slightly elongated, bead, .6-.8 cm in diameter. They are produced near branchlet ends in loose, branching small clusters and may persist for several months.

TREE-OF-HEAVEN
Ailanthus altissima

The Tree-of-Heaven was brought into California by the Chinese who came to work in the gold mines and railroads. Now it is definitely naturalized in many areas and is actively spreading by underground shoots. These young sprouts have stout, smooth, green

stems with tiny white dots, the bark turning grayish with larger definite white spots as the stem grows larger and older. In fact, you can tell where each succeeding year's growth is by the change in dot size—the dots get larger as the tree gets older and changes at each annual growth ring. The tree may grow as tall as 20 meters (60'), with the mature bark grayish-tan and irregularly or zigzag fissured.

The leaves are long and pinnately compound with 11-25 pointed leaflets. Young leaves have beautiful wine-red tip leaflets, gradually greening to the color of those at base. By the time the leaves mature they become very long—40-50 cm or even 60 cm long, (18-36''). The leaflets have one or two teeth along the margin near the base. They are broad at the base, and keep that width till past the middle, then taper to a very long narrow tip.

The flowers are small and greenish in large branching clusters at the branchlet ends, with the male and female flowers separate. The male flowers have a strong odor. The female flowers develop long, linear, simple samaras.

When the leaves drop in the fall, they leave large heart-shaped scars.

LOMBARDY POPLAR
Populus nigra italica

The Lombardy Poplar is a native of the northern part of Italy, but it is planted practically worldwide wherever there is enough water to make it grow—which it does rapidly. It is one of the fastest growing trees, and spreads by root sprouts. It produces no seeds, and propagates itself only vegetatively, but very successfully, for it can fill an area rapidly. It is most often planted for quick shade or windbreak. A tree does not live too many years—probably 25-30 in healthy condition, but the young sprouts take over when the old one dies.

It is easily recognized by its many slender branches turning abruptly upwards, paralleling the vertically fissured rough gray trunk. Thus, the silhouette is tall and slender and is a common sight

in many areas. They are often planted along roads, for their branches don't grow out and over the road.

The leaves are triangular in shape, the flattish base slightly toothed. The round-tooth sides taper quite rapidly to a sharp point. The long petiole is flattened from side to side, its flat side attached at right angles to the flat surface of the leaf blade, and so, like the Aspen and Fremont Cottonwood, the leaves will flutter in slight breezes.

LOCUST
Robinia pseudoacacia

The Locust is a common escapee tree in the west, but a native to eastern United States. It has rough, fissured, charcoal-colored bark. It grows to be quite a large, open, many-branched, attractive tree. It spreads by abundant seeds, and also by underground shoots. The leaves have 7-9 pairs of oval leaflets, or with an odd-number of leaflets with one at the tip. The soft, dull, bluish-green leaves are pinnately compound. The leaflets are either oppositely or alternately arranged, sometimes with the last pair opposite each other just at the tip, sometimes the additional single leaflet is at the tip. The upper surface of the compound leaf vein is flat with a groove down the middle; the lower side is rounded. The stipules at leaf base may be spine-like.

The white, pea-like, fragrant flowers hang in drooping clusters, each flower 1.5-2 cm. The fruit is a glossy brown pod 5-10 cm long (2-4''), which contains about a dozen seeds.

NEW MEXICAN LOCUST
Robinia neo-mexicana

The New Mexican Locust is an "intruder," and has spread widely over the southwest. It tends to be a much smaller tree than the other locusts, but produces vast amounts of flowers—which explains why it was first brought in by man, and also how it has escaped.

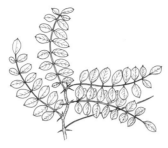

It produces many seeds from those flowers, and also spreads rapidly by underground shoots. It is now found, growing like a native, especially on cooler slopes, with Piñon Pine, Juniper and Rocky Mountain Oak and very abundantly along many roads in hilly or mountainous areas.

The pinnately compound leaves have 15-21 smooth-margined leaflets, but the stem is noticeably hairy. There are dark brown or reddish spines at the base of each leaf stem, and down along the spray.

The many pinkish to purplish flowers bloom in slender drooping spikes, and produce hairy seed pods 7-10 cm long (3-4''). The seeds are small and dark brown. The wood is very hard and strong.

This escapee is now found from southern Nevada and southeastern Utah through most of Arizona (except the southwestern parts), into southern Colorado and New Mexico (except the southeastern part), and into Mexico.

ACACIA
Acacia decurrens

The acacias are a large group of shrubs and trees belonging to the pea family. There are about 450 species, growing in warm climates, many of them have adapted to desert climates. Catclaw is a native acacia of the southwest, and various acacias has been planted, and thrive, from Texas to California, and some have escaped. The most common "Intruder" is the Black Acacia, with evergreen double-pinnately compound leaves which give the tree a very feathery appearance. They are bluish-green, from 6-10 cm long (2.25-4''), and

may lie flat and show their tiny subleaflets or may almost fold up if the air is too hot.

The tree usually produces a stout trunk and many large branches, and often puts out shoots from the base, so a cluster of trees develop. The bark is smooth and gray with purplish and/or greenish tinges.

The flowers are produced in clusters on flower stems from the leaf axis. They are brilliant yellow, fuzzy, tiny balls with many stamens, practically covering the tree. Pollen is produced in abundance (many people have trouble with hayfever during acacia-blooming time). There are many different kinds of acacias. some species have a narrow leathery "leaf"—which is really a petiole.

Many small (.4 cm) jet-black seeds are released from the 4-8 cm (1.5-3'') purplish-brown pods, which twist and spiral when dry. The empty pods may hang from their long thin stems for some time, giving the tree a definite purplish-tint.

TAMARIX
(Saltcedar)
Tamarix pentandra

Tamarix is so well established along streams and low moist areas in the southwest (and up into the central valley of California) that few people realize it is an "Intruder." It has become the dominant shrub or small tree along many rivers, and can be found up to 7,000 feet elevation, often producing thickets.

It was brought from Asia Minor, to be used as a windbreak plant. It escaped and now can be found in California, Arizona, New Mexico, and Mexico along practically all valley bottoms.

The minute leaves are scale-like along a fine, tough stem. The pink flowers are also minute, but are thickly produced along the flower stems which branch everywhere from the leaf stems. When in bloom it gives the impression of pink haze or clouds. The capsule releases many tiny seeds, each with a tuft of hairs, so the seeds are wind-carried and germinate quickly if they fall on moist ground.

Others species with darker pink flowers or more interesting growth are commonly planted in southwest gardens.

Chapter VII

HOW TO GROW NATIVE TREES
FROM SEED

Many people would like to grow their own native trees from seeds—it's not too difficult for many of them. Remember, particularly, that to make them sprout you need to give them certain conditions. This is especially true of "wintering"—a cold storage time that many mountain tree seeds naturally go through as they are covered with the winter snows, then the damp melting snow time, and finally the warm days but cool nights of spring. Other seeds, as acorns, often lie where they are covered by leaves in the autumn. Decomposition of the leaves takes place over the winter with rain and perhaps snow—and decomposition produces heat. This helps explain why you should treat acorns as suggested below.

The methods given here are ways that hopefully imitate natural conditions but "speed-up" the sprouting and perhaps increase the percentages of ones that grow by controlling the conditions.

Generally speaking, it is best to start native trees in the late fall or winter. This is the time they would naturally be "getting ready"; this gives you the time for the "speed-up" treatment, and the seed is freshest then. Seeds of maples, buckeyes, and oaks especially must be planted before they dry out.

Many seeds naturally lie dormant for a period of time because the seed coat must first break down. So for these, the "speed-up" consists of various treatments which hurry the decomposition of the seed coat.

Other seeds, particularly those of trees that live in cold winter conditions of high mountains seem to have an "internal dormancy." Until that situation is met, the seeds won't properly germinate. The easiest treatment for this is called "cold stratification." You imitate winter conditions by placing the seed in a moist soil mix or peat moss in a tightly closed plastic bag, refrigerating it for 1-3 months, and then plant right away.

Another type of "internal dormancy" is a chemical one and some seeds respond best when so treated—as placing them on activated charcoal. In natural conditions, the chemical in the seed coat is leached away by weathering.

In the following pages, suggestions are given for growing native trees from seeds. Remember always to collect the seed as soon as possible after it matures, then give it the recommended treatment. Do not let the seeds lie around—they tend to dry rapidly.

Be sure you have a place ready for the sprouting seeds after their treatment (which may be weeks or months later). Once treated, they should be planted immediately. Plant in good soil, keep moist but not wet and avoid placing them near walls where reflected heat may "bake" them.

CONIFERS:

As a general rule the conifers need to be "cold-stratified." Be sure the nuts have no holes in them (if they do, they have probably been used by an insect as food and the embryo is damaged or gone). Place seeds in plastic bag filled with moist but not wet mix of ⅓ sand, ⅓ soil, ⅓ humus. Label on the outside the name of the conifer, the date in and the date when it should be taken out of the refrigerator. Refrigerate according to the following schedule. At end of the time, remove carefully from the plastic bag (some may have started sprouting), plant seeds in deep containers—not too many to any one container. Use good soil mix; keep moist but not wet.

PINES:

Yellow Pine *(P. ponderosa)*	1½ months
Beach Pine *(P. contorta)*	1½ months
Jeffrey Pine *(P. jeffreyi)*	1½ months
Bishop Pine *(P. muricata)*	1½ months
Torrey Pine *(P. torreyana)*	1-3 months
Bristlecone *(P. aristata)*	3 months
Sugar Pine *(P. lambertiana)*	3 months

No cold stratification needed; plant immediately:
Coulter Pine *(P. coulteri)*
Western White Pine *(P. monticola)*

Monterey Pine *(P. radiata)*
Digger Pine *(P. sabiniana*)

SPRUCE:
    Engelmann *(P. engelmannii)*   no treatment needed
    Sitka *(P. sitchensis)*   2-3 months
    Weeping *(P. breweriana)*   1-3 months

HEMLOCK:
    Hemlock *(T. heterophylla*   3 months
    and *T. mertensiana)*

DOUGLAS FIR:
    Douglas Fir *(P. menziesii*   1-2 months
    and *macrocarpa)*

CYPRESS:
    Cypress   no treatment; germination often slow and unpredictable

FIR:
    Santa Lucia *(A bracteata)*   3-4 months
    White Fir *(A. concolor)*   1½ months
    Red Fir *(A. magnifica)*   1½ months
    Grand Fir *(A. grandis)*   1 month

SEQUOIA:
    Giant Sequoia *(S. gigantea)* 2½ months; partial shade first year

    Coast Redwood *(S. semper-* no treatment; partial shade
    virens)   first year

CEDAR:
    Incense Cedar *(C. decurrens)* 2 months
    Western Red Cedar *(T.*   1-2 months
    plicata)

CHAMAECYPARIS:
    Port Orford Cedar; Alaska no stratification necessary but
    Cypress *(C. lawsoniana* and 1½ months may improve ger-
    nootkatensis)   mination

NUTMEG:
    Nutmeg *(T. californica)*   3 months germination is *very* slow

BROADLEAF TREES

Cold stratification is also successful for many broadleaf or deciduous trees. The table below gives the period of time. Follow the directions as for conifers, using appropriate time. Some broadleaf trees, however also need hot water (180°) treatment. This is hotter than used for oaks. Heat the water to 180°, turn off the heat, dump in the seeds and let them sit in the cooling water for twelve hours. This gives them time to absorb water after the seed coat has been softened by the heat.

OAKS:

    Collect acorns as soon as they start dropping. Toss them into water heated to 140°, skimming off all that float—those will either be ones that did not develop or that have been eaten by insects. Leave acorns in the water till it cools, then put them in plastic bags with moist (but not wet) mixture that is ⅓ sand, ⅓ humus, ⅓ soil. Close bag tightly and put in out-of-the-way corner in the refrigerator for six weeks. Remove and plant. Remember that oaks develop a long tap root very early, so plant them in deep containers. Many of the California oaks are accustomed to a dry summer, so don't overwater the young sprouts, especially their first year. Transplant to permanent location by the second year if possible (remember that long tap root).

Alders	plant as soon as possible; no treatment
Aspen	plant fresh seed
Bay (*U. californica*)	use fresh seed; stratification (1 mo.) may improve germination; no treatment; plant immediately; keep moist
Birch	no treatment; plant immediately; keep moist
Buckeye	plant immediately; special fun to grow this one
Cascara	3 month stratification
Ceanothus	hot water, then plant
Cherry:	
Bitter	3 months
Choke	3 months
Holly-leafed	use fresh drupe; plant immediately

Dogwood	use fresh seed; stratification (1½ months) improves germination
Fremontia	hot water (180°) and 2-3 months stratification
Hazelnut	2-3 months stratification
Indigo Bush	no treatment
Madrone	3 months stratification; when ready to plant, plant can and all—does not tolerate root disturbance; can will rust away
Maples:	
Vine	2 months stratification
Mountain	3 months stratification
Big-leaf	3 months stratification
Redbud	180° water plus 2 months stratification
Sycamore	2-3 months stratification
Silk-tassel	3 months stratification
Tanbark Oak	no treatment; use fresh seed, plant immediately
Toyon	plant fresh seed
Willow	stem cuttings; use fresh twigs, place in moist sand, keep damp

Glossary

Achene: Small, dry, one-seeded fruit which doesn't break open

Acorn: Fruit of an oak. A nut with a point, sitting in a scaly cup

Acute: Sharp-pointed

Axil: Angle between the leaf and the twig

Alternate: Type of arrangement, first on one side, then on other side

Berry: A fleshy 1- to several-seeded fruit

Blade: (of leaf): The flat, expanded part

Bloom: A white waxy coating (especially as applied to juniper berries)

Bract: A modified leaf or part of a cone. Especially noticeable protruding beyond the cone scales of Douglas Fir

Bristle: A stiff, hair-like structure (as on tips of Black Oak leaf)

Bur: A spiny fruit

Catkin: A small scaly spike or spike-like flower cluster, usually hanging; petals often missing or very small (as in oaks, birches)

Chaparral: Referring to areas of typical, stiff, shrubby growth

"Closed Cone": Refers to pines whose cones remain closed even after maturity. They may open if removed from the tree or if tree dies, or in some cases, not till after a fire goes through area

Compound leaf: A leaf composed of 2 or more distinct parts of leaflets

Concave: Bowed in the form of an arch

Convex: Opposite of concave

Deciduous: Not persistent, e.g. leaves fall in the autumn

Double-pinnately compound: Each leaflet of a pinnately compound leaf is divided into leaflets (i.e., each pinna is divided into pinnules)

Drupe: Fruit with a stone or pit inside a fleshy outer part

Entire: Refers to margin of leaf that is smooth, with no teeth or lobes

Evergreen: Persistent. Refers to trees that do not drop leaves in the autumn but stay green during the winter

Gall: A swelling of plant tissue usually due to fungi or insect parasites

Gland: A structure which secretes, often appearing as a small bump

Hybridize: A cross between two different species

Involuere: One or more whorls of bracts situated below and close to a flower, flower cluster, or fruit

Leaflets: The divisions of a leaf which has many parts; i.e.—a division of a compound leaf

Midrib: Central or main rib of a leaf

Node: The place on the stem where a leaf arises

Nut: A hard shelled, 1-seeded fruit; doesn't open by itself

Opposite: A type of arrangement. Located at same level on stem, across from each other

Palmately compound: Leaflets arranged like palm of a hand, all beginning at a common center

Palmately veined: Veins arranged like palm of a hand, all beginning at a common center

Petiole: Stalk or stem of a leaf

Pinna: The first division or leaflet of a compound leaf. (pl) pinnae

Pinnately compound: Pinnae (or leaflets) arranged on each side along stem of compound leaf

Pinnately veined: Veins arising one after another along each side of the main vein

Pinnule: A division of a pinna. Double-pinnately compound leaves have pinnae divided into pinnules

Pistil: The female part of the flower, including the ovary where seeds develop

Pod: A dry fruit that breaks open

Pubescent: Hairy, especially if soft or downy

Raceme: Flower cluster with pedicels all about the same length

Rachis: The "mid-stem" of a pinnately compound leaf—i.e., the leaflets are arranged along the rachis

Samara: A winged, non-opening fruit as in ashes. Maples have double samaras

Sepal: The outer envelope of a flower—usually green; covers flower while in bud

Serpentine: A mineral or rock that usually has a dull green color and often a mottled appearance, generally found along a fault zone

Serrate: Toothed, may be fine to coarse

Sessile: Sits on something with no petiole or stem (as a sessile leaf right on twig)

Simple (leaf): A single leaf, perhaps lobed, but not divided into leaflets

Spike: Cluster of sessile flowers arranged along the flower stem

Stamen: The male part of a flower, the upper part being the anther which produces pollen

Stigma: The receptive part of the pistil

Stipule: Small appendages at base of leaf petiole, usually in pairs

Stomates: Breathing pores in leaves; often appear as white dots or bands of whiteness, especially in conifers

Tannin: Substance used in tanning, dyeing, making ink, and in medicine

Umbo: The raised spur or "nose" in center of scale or cone (especially of pine or cypress)

Bibliography

Abrams, LeRoy. *Illustrated Flora of the Pacific States*. Stanford, California: Stanford University Press, Vol. 1, 1940; Vol. 2, 1944; Vol. 3, 1951; Vol. 4 by Raxana Ferris, 1960.

Arno, Stephen F. *Discovering Sierra Trees*. Yosemite Natural History Association and Sequoia Natural History Association in cooperation with the National Park Service, 1973.

Berry, James Berthold. *Western Forest Trees; a guide to the identification of trees and wood for students, teachers, farmers and woodsmen*. New York: Dover, 1964.

Bowers, N. A. *Cone-bearing Trees of the Pacific Coast*. Palo Alto; Pacific Book, 1961.

Collingwood, George Harris. *Knowing Your Trees*. Rev. & ed. by Devereux Butcher. American Forestry Assn., 1964.

Geary, Ida. *The Leaf Book: Field Guide to Plants of Northern California*. Fairfax, California: A Philpott, 1972.

Jepson, Willis Linn. *A Manual of the Flowering Plants of California*. rev. ed. Berkeley: University of California Press, 1960.

Kearney, Thomas H. and Robert H. Peebles. *Arizona Flora*. 2nd Edition, Berkeley: University of California Press, 1960.

Lamb, Samuel H. *Woody Plants of the Southwest; a field guide with descriptive text, drawings, range maps and photographs*. Santa Fe, New Mexico: Sunstone Press, 1975.

Little, Elbert L. Jr. *Atlas of United States Trees.* Vol. 1: *Conifers and Important Hardwoods.* U.S. Department of Agriculture. Miscellaneous Publication #1146, 1971.

Metcalf, Woodbridge. *Native Trees of the San Francisco Bay Region*. Berkeley: University of California Press, 1959.

Munz, Philip A. *A California Flora*. Berkeley: University of California Press, 1959; Supplement, 1968.

Nelson, Dick and Sharon. *Easy Field Guide to Common Trees of Arizona*. Glenwood, New Mexico: Tecolote Press, 1976.

Nelson, Ruth Elizabeth. *Handbook of Rocky Mountain Plants*. D. S. King, 1969.

Peattie, Donald Culross. *A Natural History of Western Trees*. New York: Bonanza Books, Crown Publishers, 1953.

Peterson, Peter Victor. *Native Trees of Southern California*. Berkeley: University of California Press, 1966.

_____,*Native Trees of the Sierra Nevada*. Berkeley: University of California Press, 1975.

Storer, Tracy I, and Robert L. Usinger. *Sierra Nevada Natural History*. Berkeley: University of California Press, 1966. pp. 140–164.

Sudworth, George Bishop. *Forest Trees of the Pacific Slope*. Dover, 1967.

United States Department of Agriculture. *The Yearbook of Agriculture, 1949. Trees*. Government Printing Office, 1949. pp. 799–814.

Watts, May Theilgaard and Tom Watts. *Desert Tree Finder: a pocket manual for identifying desert trees*. Berkeley: Nature Study Guild, 1974.

Watts, Tom. *Pacific Coast Tree Finder: a pocket manual for identifying Pacific Coast trees*. Berkeley: Nature Study Guild, 1973.

Watts, Tom. *Rocky Mountain Tree Finder; a pocket manual for identifying Rocky Mountain trees*. Berkeley: Nature Study Guild, 1972.

INDEX